# SUTTEE

# SUTTEE:

## A HISTORICAL AND PHILOSOPHICAL ENQUIRY INTO THE HINDU RITE OF WIDOW-BURNING

EDWARD THOMPSON

GYAN

*Published by*

GYAN

Gyan Publishing House
5, Ansari Road
Daryaganj, New Delhi-110002
Phone: 011-47034999, 9811692060
E-mail: books@gyanbooks.com

*Distribution Network*
gyanbooks.com
India, USA, Canada, UK, Australia



ISBN: 978-93-6920-083-2 (PB)

First Published, 1928

2nd Impression 2025

*Printed at:* Gyan Press, Delhi.



**SUTTEE**
Author: EDWARD THOMPSON

# SUTTEE

*BY THE SAME AUTHOR*

VERSE

Via Triumphalis
Selected Poems

DRAMA

Krishna Kumari
Atonement
Three Eastern Plays (with Theodosia Thompson)

FICTION

Cithaeron Dialogues
An Indian Day
These Men Thy Friends

HISTORY

The Other Side of the Medal
A History of India (Benn's Sixpenny Library)

"SATI" MEMORIALS ON THE ROAD TO HAMPI

# SUTTEE

## A HISTORICAL AND PHILOSOPHICAL ENQUIRY INTO THE HINDU RITE OF WIDOW-BURNING

BY

EDWARD THOMPSON

BOSTON AND NEW YORK
HOUGHTON MIFFLIN COMPANY
The Riverside Press, Cambridge
1928

"THIS last proof of the perfect unity of body and soul, this devotion beyond the grave, has been chosen by many of our Western critics as our reproach; we differ from them in thinking of our 'suttees' not with pity, but with understanding, respect, and love. So far from being ashamed of our 'suttees,' we take a pride in them; that is even true of the most 'progressive' amongst us. It is very much like the tenderness which our children's children may some day feel for those of their race who were willing to throw away their lives for 'their country, right or wrong,' though the point of view may seem to us then, as it seems to so many of us already, evidence rather of generosity than balanced judgment. . . . For some reason it has come to be believed that Sati must have been a man-made institution [1] imposed on women by men for reasons of their own, that it is associated with feminine servility, and that it is peculiar to India. We shall see that these views are historically unsound. It is true that in aristocratic circles Sati became to some degree a social convention, and pressure was put on unwilling individuals, precisely as conscripts are even now forced to suffer or die for other people's ideas; and from this point of view we cannot but be glad that it was prohibited by law in 1829 on the initiative of Raja Rammohun Roy. But now that nearly a century has passed, it should not be difficult to review the history and significance of Sati more dispassionately than was possible in the hour of controversy and the atmosphere of religious prejudice."—ANANDA COOMARASWAMY, *The Dance of Siva*, published 1924, 91–2.

"The devotion of Alcestis! Assuredly the heroic unselfishness of woman is a beautiful thing; and I warrant you that, the gods helping me, Alcestis shall take no injury from my hands. But what of Admetus as a husband? That is an aspect of the matter upon which our hymnists and our

[1] Author's note: "'Social conventions' are rarely '*man*-made laws' alone."

congregations are little disposed to dwell, and they find no difficulty in ignoring it. It belongs to the skimble-skamble thinking which aids and is aided by faith in these monstrosities never to see anything steadily, never to see anything *whole*, but only such parts as please. And your heroic tragedy is beloved for flattering this habit. But there are flatterers enough; and, for my part, I intend to give you much more of Admetus than of Alcestis. He is much better for you. You are accustomed to rest with complacency on the picture of the self-sacrificing woman as the ideal of wives. For herself she deserves such admiration, but for men and for society, no! I should like to make you feel, and I mean to try, what a blind, barbarous, self-defeating selfishness is at the bottom of all this rapture about the devotion of woman. You will say that the women join in it. But what sort of women? What are the women bred by our system of semi-humanity but the most dangerous of our slaves? Prohibited by your generosity from acquiring intelligence except at the cost of respect, the poor creatures are so dull that they cannot even distinguish a friend from an enemy. Your magnanimous satirists have no difficulty in directing the almost unanimous resentment of the sex against whoever dares to see and show what mischief to themselves and to us results from their ill-governed virtue not less than from their ungoverned vice. I pity Alcestis, and I pity her husband. What would she make of him? What *does* she make of him?"—A. W. VERRALL, *Euripides the Rationalist*, 118–19 (Euripides is supposed to be speaking).

'It is a strange commentary on the magnanimity of men that they should seek their deliverance through the self-sacrifice of their wives."—AKBAR, quoted by ABUL FAZL in *Happy Sayings of His Majesty* (*Ain-i-Akbari, Institutes of Akbar*), Jarret, iii. 398.

# PREFACE

I SUPPOSE the impulse to write this book dates back to my shame and anger in India when men and women of my own race extolled suttee, and the amazement with which I first saw the memorials of Hindu kings, with the *satīs'* crouching forms. But the impulse was slight, and would have slept but for a publisher's interest. Messrs. Allen & Unwin passed on to me questions asked about suttee by their reader when reporting on my share in *Three Eastern Plays*. Receiving my reply, they suggested that I should write an *Essay on Suttee*. I said I would; but the essay at once got out of hand and became a monograph. I found with surprise how slight was the attention given in any language, Indian or European, to the subject, and how loose and erroneous were many statements of even the best historians. Our ignorance of what is commonplace and pervading in the atmosphere and background of Indian thought justified the slight terminal essay that appeared as an appendix to *Three Eastern Plays*; but the necessity was unfortunate, for reviewers assumed an afterthought as a first cause, and said the plays were about—or even against—suttee.

The late Lieutenant-Colonel C. Eckford Luard, C.I.E., helped me with discussion and information. His death was as heavy a loss as any that Indian scholarship has suffered in recent years, and to his friends a thing hard to be borne.

The picture of Chitor is reproduced from Tod's *Rajasthan*, by courtesy of the Clarendon Press; the other three illustrations are reproduced from Government of India publications, by courtesy of the High Commissioner for India. I acknowledge these favours gratefully. Part of Chapters VI to VIII appeared in the London and Edinburgh Quarterlies.

Except when a misspelling was so well established that accuracy would have been pedantry, I have used the orthography accepted by scholars. But the authorities whom I quote made shots at transliteration which resulted in a wide range of variation. My printers, noting this, have been at pains to correct many of these mistakes; and I have been too tolerant, when they have done this, to restore the false spelling of my original.

# CONTENTS

# ILLUSTRATIONS

# SUTTEE

## CHAPTER I

## ORIGIN OF SUTTEE

### SUTTEE AND THE HINDU SCRIPTURES.

THE rite by which a Hindu widow became *satī*, "faithful," had two forms: *sahamaraṇa*, "dying in company with," and *anumaraṇa*, "dying in accordance with." The latter was the term used when her lord died and was burned at a distance from her—during a campaign perhaps, or when her own death was postponed because she was pregnant; she was then burned with something that belonged to and represented her husband—his shoes or turban or some piece of clothing. *Sahamaraṇa* and *anumaraṇa* were sometimes called *sahagamana*, "going along with," and *anugamana*. There were other names for the rite, local or less usual. *Satī* is the term used of the woman, and never of the rite; its application in the latter sense is modern and European.

> "We have not found the term exactly in any European document older than Sir C. Malet's letter of 1787 and Sir W. Jones's letter of the same year." [1]

For convenience, I intend to use throughout this

[1] Sir H. Yule and A. C. Burnell, *Hobson-Jobson*, article "Suttee."

book *satī* for the person who commits this form of ceremonial suicide, and the anglicized form "suttee" for the act itself.

*Anumaraṇa* had its drawbacks in a land and age of rumours hastily accepted for truth. Instances are on record of widows hearing that their husbands had died while away from home and burning themselves a few days before their safe return. It was forbidden to women of the Brahman caste, and, although this rule was freely transgressed, especially in Bengal, its existence was ascertained by the British Government, who prohibited this kind of suicide by Brahmanis in 1817, twelve years before suttee itself was prohibited altogether.

Suttee is ancient; but, as a Hindu rite, not of the greatest antiquity. The *Rig-Veda* very fully presents the funeral ceremonies of the Aryans, but contains only one or two lines that *may*, on a dubious twisting and loosening of their natural meaning, glance at suttee. The one line which was held to enjoin it clearly was shown by Professor Wilson[1] to have been deliberately changed; and Max Müller says of it that it was "mangled, mistranslated, and misapplied."[2] There was certainly suspicion of its untrustworthiness, if not full knowledge, long before European scholars revealed it, for, in the thirty years of vacillation before the British Government

[1] See *Essays and Lectures Chiefly on the Religion of the Hindus*, by H. H. Wilson, 1862, ii. 270–292.

[2] *Selected Essays on Language, Mythology, and Religion* (1881), i. 335.

dared to suppress suttee, Hindu pundits were continually asked for their opinion, and rarely cared to say more than that suttee was recommended, but not actually commanded, by their shastras. Rammohan Ray treated the alleged shastric support with a verbal respect that thinly veiled his contempt for it.

The original text ran:

> *Ārohantu janayo yonim agre*
>
> (Let the mothers advance to the altar first.)

By a change of two letters, of *agre* to *agneḥ*, the genitive of *agni*, " fire," the line became:

> *Ārohantu janayo yonim agneḥ*
>
> (Let the mothers go into the womb of fire.)

Max Müller calls this celebrated change of text " perhaps the most flagrant instance of what can be done by an unscrupulous priesthood."[1] The tag, *Tantum religio potuit suadere malorum*, comes to mind. Yet, to be fair, we should probably have to substitute for *religio* whatever is the Latin equivalent for " literary conscience." For, though the change from *agre* to *agneḥ* is almost certainly proved both by context and by reference to the early Hindu commentators on the *Rig-Veda*, yet in the uncontaminated passage the word *yoni* is used with a looseness of

[1] *Selected Essays on Language, Mythology, and Religion* (1881), i. 335.

meaning that a purist would dislike. That meaning is secondary and careless, like the meaning put upon *nice*, in "a nice cake" or "a nice girl." The man who changed *agre* to *agneḥ* was three parts pedant to one part bigot, and the change illustrates the extent to which a thoroughly scholarly mind is prepared to go to get a satisfactory reading.

The original text had no reference to widows or to suttee, but was an injunction laid on all the mothers present. G. U. Pope has a comment similar to Max Müller's: "Few false readings have had consequences so fearful!"[1] But widow-burning, though the comment is justified, cannot have been established by this change of text, but only encouraged. It must have had already a vogue which demanded that support in the earliest scriptures be found for it. And the change must have been a comparatively late one, for though the *Atharva-Veda* has texts enjoining suttee, in other sacred books, ancient but (like the *Atharva-Veda*) admittedly much later than the *Rig-Veda*, the examples of widow-burning cited are few and plainly exceptional. In the *Mahābhārata*, one of the two widows of Pandu is, after a lengthy argument between her and her co-wife as to which is entitled to the privilege, allowed as a high honour to share her husband's pyre. Four of Krishna's wives and four of Vasudeva's burned on their lord's death. But "after the great war in Kuru-kshetra

[1] Dubois (second edition, 1879), 180.

none of the numerous royal ladies burned herself." [1] The *Rāmāyana* is free from suttee. The lawgiver Manu, commending it, does not command it. Such scriptural support as Hinduism gave the rite is mainly in the much later *Purāṇas*, where we find the legend of Kali as *satī*, the faithful wife who slew herself in grief for an insult to her lord Siva. The few instances in the *Mahābhārata* are later interpolations. "The much-abused *Tantras* forbid it." [2]

When the attention of the British Government was first seriously drawn to the rite, it was so entrenched by centuries of performance that the enquiry as to whether Hindu scriptures enjoined it was irrelevant and useless. It was as well established as the habit of warfare in Christian Europe. Nevertheless, the enquiry had a value, if only because it helped to encourage the Government at last to break through its timidity and past its promises of toleration for all religious rites. This rite was not only obviously immoral and wicked, it was also not essential to Hinduism.

## ORIGIN OF THE RITE.

By the fourth century B.C. Alexander's soldiers found suttee prevalent in the Panjab, and

"that it was practised by the half-foreign city of Taxila

[1] Balfour, *Cyclopædia of India*, article "Suttee."

[2] Sir Charles Eliot, *Hinduism and Buddhism*, ii. 168.

along with other startling customs, and that it also prevailed among the Kathaioi, who dwelt on the banks of the Ravi." [1]

Western scholars often ascribe suttee to "Scythian" influence. Thus Vincent Smith says:

> "The scanty evidence as to Taxilan institutions taken as a whole suggests that the civilization of the people was compounded of various elements—Babylonian, Iranian, Scythian and Vedic. Suttee probably was a Scythian rite introduced from Central Asia." [2]

And again:

> "There can be little doubt that the suttee rite was brought into India by early immigrants over the north-western passes," [3]

brought from what the author has just styled

> "tribes in Central and Western Asia, and even in Eastern Europe, who may be called Scythians in a general way."

This "Scythian" theory is adopted by most writers who refer to suttee, following the *Oxford History*. But the theory dates back to Tod's famous *Annals and Antiquities of Rajasthan*.

Herodotus [4] says that the Scythians, at the burial of their kings, used to kill, embalm, and bury in the barrow fifty youths on fifty horses, along with the king's cup-bearer, cook, groom, lackey, messenger, and "one of his concubines." But there is only the slightest resemblance [5] between this holocaust of a

[1] Vincent A. Smith, *Oxford History of India*, 665.

[2] *Ibid.*, 62. [3] *Ibid.*, 665. [4] iv. 71–73.

[5] An exception must be made for Rajasthan and adjacent territory, where male slaves were often burnt as well as female ones.

king's entire range of possessions (golden vessels and trinkets and robes included) and Hindu suttee. There is a nearer resemblance between suttee and Thracian funeral rites.

"Each man among them has several wives; and no sooner does a man die than a sharp contest ensues among the wives upon the question which of them all the husband loved most tenderly. The friends of each eagerly plead on her behalf, and she to whom the honour is adjudged, after receiving the praises both of men and women, is slain over the grave by the hand of her next of kin, and then buried with her husband. The others are sorely grieved, for nothing is considered such a disgrace." [1]

There is no evidence that suttee was introduced from "Scythia," or from anywhere outside India—introduced, that is, *after* the Vedic period, which is what the *Oxford History* implies. If it had been so introduced, it would have been under brahmanical sanction; but the Brahmans, while presiding at the sacrifice and drawing fees from it and in every way supporting it, kept a memory that it was not a rite to which their own women were liable, and invented a text which, while enjoining it for other castes, forbade it to Brahmanis. Dubois writes in 1816:

"The Brahman women no longer continue the practice of burning themselves alive with the bodies of their husbands. This custom is relinquished to other castes, as well as many others which require the endurance of bodily pain." [2]

---

[1] Herodotus, v. 5 (translated by George Rawlinson).

[2] *Manners and Customs of the People of India* (1879 edition), 174. Suttee is forbidden to Brahmanis in the *Bṛhaddevatā*, which leaves it open for other castes. "With regard to the other castes, this law for women may be or may not be."

Dubois' statement holds chiefly of Southern India, for Brahman women burnt freely enough in Bengal and Rajasthan to a much later date than 1816. Yet it is likely that the women of this caste did, even in Bengal and Rajasthan, enjoy some measure of immunity from the rite.

Suttee was a custom to glorify the warrior caste, and especially princes. It would have been strange if the Aryans when living in Central Asia had refrained from copying their neighbours "the Scythians," and yet, centuries later, when long settled in India, had imported the rite from a people now at least a thousand miles away. But, though we must reject this theory of a later borrowing, the mere silence of the *Rig-Veda* must not be pressed so far as to be held to *prove* that suttee was unknown to, or even among, the Aryan invaders. Sir Charles Eliot states the utmost that those who assert that the rite existed in Vedic times are entitled to claim—the evidence being against the claim, but not so conclusively as to make his qualified form of it impossible:

> 'Even in the Vedic age the custom had been discontinued as barbarous" (i.e. it *had* been in vogue, was still a memory and perhaps an occasional practice). "But even at this period those who did not follow the Vedic customs may have killed widows with their husbands; and later the invaders from Central Asia probably reinforced the usage." [1]

In the Vedic funeral rites the widow lay by her husband on the pyre. But, immediately after the

[1] *Hinduism and Buddhism,* ii. 168.

*Arohantu janayo yonim agre*

(Let the mothers advance to the altar first),

the hymn continues with the exhortation:

> "Rise up, woman, come to the world of living beings; thou sleepest nigh unto the lifeless. Come; thou hast been associated with maternity through the husband by whom thy hand was formerly taken.
>
> "Taking his bow from the hand of the dead, that it may be to us for help. . . ." [1]

As the widow descended from the pyre the dead man's friends took from his hand the symbol of his caste, whether Brahman, Kshatriya, or Vaisya (priest, warrior, or merchant)—a piece of gold, a bow, or a jewel. The leader [2] of the Hindu party who asserted in the nineteenth century the Vedic sanction of suttee interpreted these words thus:

> "If the widow thus addressed has not made up her mind for her immolation, she obeys the call; but should she be firm in her resolve, she consoles her friends and relatives and enters the fire." [3]

The plain interpretation of the text is that she returns to the world of the living; and I suppose no scholar of repute would now maintain that suttee was a Vedic rite.

The rite was almost certainly, in my judgment, indigenous to India, along with human sacrifice and other primitive cruelties, when the Aryans entered

[1] H. H. Wilson, *Essays*, ii. 272.

[2] Raja Radhakanta Deb. See Wilson, *Essays*, ii. 293–305

[3] Wilson, *Essays*, 297.

the land. They found it flourishing among the savage clans of Central India, the clans from whom they later borrowed the goddess Kali and a whole wilderness of malignant godlings and superstitions, and it was taken into Hinduism along with the people who tenaciously clung to it. Later invasions from Central Asia may have "reinforced the usage"; the Rajputs, who practised suttee on such an awful scale and relinquished it so late and unwillingly—who also often sacrificed male slaves on the pyres of their kings—represent immigrations later [1] than the Aryan ones, and from more barbaric tribes. This fact allows for the entrance of the "Scythian" theory, but by a different door from that indicated by Vincent Smith.

Widow-sacrifice was once almost universal. Grimm states [2] that it was a custom of the Scandinavian peoples; the legend of Balder, in which Nanna ascends his pyre, kept a memory of it, as did the Norse versions of the *Volsunga Saga*, which make Brünhild a *satī*. The rite was Slavonic also, and

> "the practice of burning the living widow with the corpse of the husband is stated to have been an ancient Indo-Germanic custom, based upon the belief that life in the next world is a reflex of this life." [3]

---

[1] Some at least two millenniums later.

[2] Quoted by N. M. Penzer (1926), in *Terminal Essay on Suttee*, vol. iv of C. H. Tawney's *Ocean of Story*. I have drawn upon his summary of the evidence of the ancient, almost universal prevalence of widow-sacrifice, but I have supplemented it from many other sources.

[3] N. M. Penzer, *Suttee*, 255.

In Greek legend, Evadne, wife of Capaneus, one of the Seven Against Thebes, burned with her husband; some of the accounts of Œnone made her do the same with her false lover Paris, accounts which Tennyson adopted in his *Death of Œnone,* a poem coloured by Anglo-Indian accounts of suttee. We have seen it in Thrace, as well as in Scythia; and the visitor to Luxor can see it still as it was practised in Ancient Egypt, the most humane (with the exception of Athens) of the countries of antiquity. The tomb of Amen-hetep II, the one king whose body is still *in situ,* has in an adjoining chamber to the one in which the king lies four embalmed bodies of slaughtered wives—the guide switches on the electric light and reveals them huddled there.

> ' Such customs, however, seem to have belonged to the early dynasties, and it is only with bloodthirsty rulers like Amen-hetep II that the old customs were revived." [1]

Widow-sacrifice used to exist among the Tongans and Fijians and Maoris,[2] and in many African tribes. There were relics of it in the funeral custom of some American Indian tribes, which required the widow to lie beside her husband on the pyre, as in Vedic ritual, till the smoke began to be suffocating, when she might escape. In China re-marriage of widows

[1] N. M. Penzer, *Suttee,* 256.

[2] *Old New Zealand,* by a Pakeha Maori (F. E. Maning), 1863, 218 ff.

"was always looked upon as an act of unchastity, while those who committed suicide at their husband's death had honorary gateways . . . erected in their honour by Imperial command."[1]

In fact, the rite belongs to a barbaric stratum which once overlay the world, including India. That barbaric stratum in India kept its first texture of fierce cruelty longest in the mountainous tract running across the centre of the land, from the Rajput fastnesses to the wooded hills of Orissa and the rocky jungles where the Vindhyas crumble down in Bihar.

To sum up: this relic of once widely spread savagery had sunk into desuetude among the Aryans, or their hymns would have contained clear and full mention of it—the burning of the widow would hardly have been a less important and interesting incident than the bringing of the sacrificial butter or the holy *kuśa*-grass. The rite came in with tribes taken into Hinduism, and its performance became common; and it survived till within living memory, practised by a people in many respects highly civilized and genuinely, though capriciously, humane. The Vedic religion so changed, from being an imaginative animism and nature-worship—a brook which, though we need not exaggerate its depth or the purity of its waters, was at any rate open to the sunlight and air—into a densely overgrown quag of polytheism, magic, and blood-stained superstition, that we need

[1] Penzer, *Suttee*.

not wonder at finding the grossest cruelty ruling in the far-off descendants of a people once entitled to the praise of comparative gentleness. Other religions have suffered a similar change; but I think that no religion, not even Christianity in its days of frantic bigotry and of massacre of heretics and witches, so completely changed to malignancy as Hinduism did. Both religions admittedly kept their islands of nobler belief and practice: the monastic orders during the long period when they were the most civilizing element in Europe, and the Indian forest-sages—these have enriched both the social and personal ideals of mankind. But there is very little in the official religions that does not depress the thinker who wishes to keep faith in his race.

CHAPTER II

# PREVALENCE AND AREA OF THE RITE: SUTTEE MEMORIALS

THE custom was "notorious and well established in the Panjab in the fourth century B.C.," [1] but we may take it that it was not confined to the Panjab. There is an almost unbroken chain of foreign reference to the rite, from Alexander's time to our own day; it includes Strabo, Propertius, St. Jerome, Marco Polo, and travellers from Mahommadan lands as well as Christian. From the sixteenth century to the early decades of the nineteenth we have many scores of accounts of suttee by eye-witnesses; it was not an event that a visitor could for long escape noticing. Yet "the rite was never universal, either in all parts of India, nor was it ever regarded as obligatory on all widows." [2] However, as Vincent Smith goes on to say, "the sacrifice was often, and especially in the case of princes, compulsory, so that scores or hundreds of women might be, and actually were, burnt at the funeral of a single Raja, with or without their consent." As Mr. Coomaraswamy absurdly puts it, "It is true that in aristocratic circles Sati became to some degree a social convention, and pressure was

[1] *Oxford History of India*, 665. [2] *Ibid.*

put on unwilling individuals."[1] It is hard to think of it as anything but compulsory in certain parts of India—but I shall return to this question.

The rite was an apanage of rank, but was fostered and spread by priestly influence.

> "It was introduced into Southern India with the brahmanical civilization, and was prevalent there chiefly in the strictly brahmanical kingdom of Vijayanagar and among the Mahrattas. In Malabar, the most primitive part of South India, the rite is forbidden."[2]

In Malabar a matriarchal system prevailed, which may account for the absence of the rite.

The Marathas are generally included among those who practised suttee greatly, but this is a mistake. They rendered the rite a fluctuating and unsteady allegiance; perhaps the only Hindu principalities that attempted to prohibit it before the British prohibition were Maratha ones. In the eighteenth century suttee became fairly frequent at Poona, but even then it remained *comparatively* infrequent. The suttees at the death of Marathas of the higher rank are remarkably few. Only one wife of Sivaji[3] became *satī*, and one of Rajaram, his son. The masterful Queen of Raja Shahu was compelled to burn for political reasons, to get her out of the way. The main homes of the rite were the Ganges Valley, the Panjab, Rajasthan, and, in South India, Madura and Vijayanagar.

[1] *The Dance of Siva*, 92. [2] *Hobson-Jobson*, article "Suttee."
[3] Sivaji died in 1680, Rajaram in 1700, Shahu in 1749.

The extent to which suttee prevailed in Central India especially is brought home by the innumerable *satī*-stones. There is considerable variety in the form these memorials take. Many are just upstanding stones marked with a woman's hand, often a vermilioned hand. The *satī*, setting out to die, marked the lintel of her home with her hand, freshly stained with the red stain that decks the bride. Sometimes the stain was a saffron one, such as General Hervey found at Bikanir.

> "Each luckless woman was required, by way of sealing her 'determination' to immolate herself, to place the palm of her right hand upon some yellow daub presented to her in a platter as she passed out, and to press it against the wall of the gateway, the hand-mark thus left being subsequently cut out in the wall, or, as in some instances, a hand was fashioned in marble from the model afforded by the impression and fixed upon it." [1]

Many of these hands still decorate houses. General Hervey, in 1879, counted thirty-seven that were still distinct on the Bikanir palace, where he saw many others that had faded or were too low down to be clearly seen.

Stones marked with a woman's hand were erected where suttees occurred, and exist in thousands of villages still. Especially in the Maratha country, these stones sometimes carry the sculpture of two feet (the *pādukā*), or of a foot and an arm. They are often marked with the sun and moon, to signify the

[1] General Charles Hervey, *Some Records of Crime* (1892), i. 217

eternal endurance of the memorial. In Mandi, a Himalayan Panjab state, the *satī's* memorial is a cairn [1] on which the passer-by tosses his own contribution, to placate the ghost that is still at large. In other Himalayan districts—Kulu, for example—cairns and sculptured stones stand side by side.[2] In Gujarat also we sometimes have the mere cairn:

> ' Unhewn stones, smeared with red-lead, or heaps . . . loosely thrown together." [3]

In Bengal often nothing remains but a venerated patch of ground, without any stone. I knew one such in the jungles of ruined Vishnupur, a piece of slightly raised ground, uncultivated and believed to be uncultivable, known as *Pati-ghātinī-satī-kuṇḍa*, " the firepit of the faithful wife who killed her lord." [4] There is another midway between Bankura and Chhatna, a confused mass of rock called *Sinduri-pāhāḍa*, " Vermilion Hill." To the last place a blurred legend attaches, which I am satisfied is that of a half-forgotten suttee.

But many memorials are more elaborate. At some shrines—never, I think, in Bengal—there is a larger stone or a small building engraved with the figure of the *satīs'* lord on horseback, with spear and

[1] G. T Vigne, *Travels in Kashmir, Ladak, Iskardo.*
[2] See *Indian Antiquary*, 1875, 64.
[3] A. K. Forbes, *Ras Mala* (1878 edition), 691.
[4] See " The Clouded Mirror " (*Three Eastern Plays*, by Edward and Theodosia Thompson)

armour; his *satīs* are usually ranged below him. The commonest of the more pretentious funeral monuments are raised platforms beneath a stone canopy; these are found throughout Northern India. On the platform is a stone whose sides are sometimes embossed with the wedded life of the chieftain that it commemorates; his wives are serving him, one *satī* walks before his horse with a fly-whisk, another (on another side) holds an umbrella over him. And so on.

A few descriptions will further show the range of variation:

"Engraved head-stones, either standing alone or covered by the pavilions called *chutrees*, and not unfrequently temples of greater or less size which enclose an image of the Dev. The sculptured monuments are called 'paleeyos.' They bear a rude representation of the deceased warrior mounted upon his war-horse, or driving his chariot, according to the circumstances which may have attended his fall. The *paleeyo* of the Sutee is distinguished by a woman's hand adorned with marriage bracelets."[1] (In Gujarat.)

"The deceased is also represented on the slab, riding on horseback, horse and man finely ornamented; and in front of and behind this principal form, or in rows under it, are also engraved the figures, each with arms crossed over the bosom, of the poor creatures who became the dead man's suttees on the occasion."[2] (In Rajasthan.)

"As a rule, a sculptured representation of the widow or widows who committed *satī* is carved on the stone memorial to the dead husband. . . . This type of memorial is generally known as a *virakal* or hero-stone, and in Southern India

[1] A. K. Forbes, *Ras Mala* (1856), 691. The *Dev* (literally, *God*) is the Hero whom the shrine commemorates.

[2] C. R. W. Hervey, *Some Records of Crime*, i. 211.

"SATĪ" MEMORIAL IN FRONT OF THE JAINA TEMPLE BY THE RIVER, HAMPI

they appear to have been set up chiefly in honour of feudal chiefs and nobles of the Vijayanagar empire who were slain in battle or killed in some hunting expedition. Some of these memorials, however, were set up mainly in honour of those who committed *satī*, and these . . . are generally sculptured with a pointed pillar or post, from which projects a woman's right arm, bent upwards at the elbow. The hand is raised, with fingers erect, and a lime-fruit is usually shown placed between the thumb and forefinger. This is what is alluded to in the old inscriptions, where women are said to 'have given arm and hand' . . ."[1]

Mr. Longhurst reproduces examples of both kinds of Vijayanagar memorial. The *vīrakāl* has an upper and a lower panel. The lower holds the Hero and his two *satīs*, with an elephant (to show that the former was a man of rank) in charge of an attendant. The upper shows the three spirits arrived in Vishnu's Paradise; they stand before the conch and discus, his emblems, which Garuda (his vehicle, the kite demigod) and Hanuman (the monkey-god, the attendant of Vishnu as Rama) are adoring.

Many suttee-stones have been photographed by the Indian Archæological Department, but, though undoubtedly objects of historical and antiquarian interest, they are so very many, strewn throughout an enormous tract of country, that it is not worth while reproducing them indefinitely. All the way up to the plateau where ruined Chitor lies amid jungle these witnesses are by the wayside; the plateau itself abounds with them. Above the women's

[1] A. H. Longhurst, *Hampi Ruins*, 38.

bathing-place is the *Mahāsatī*, "the Great Place of Faithfulness," with the monuments of kings and nobles. To the spectator of any imagination the place is grim to the point of oppression. Above are the city's mighty battlements, and the flashing colour of the wild parrots and peacocks that abound here; below is the cool, secluded place of waters, collecting in a perfect bathing-pool before plunging in a long shining arrow to the plain. Here thousands of women bathed for the last time before going to their lord's funeral pile, and here ended the secret corridor from palace to pool—the corridor that leads to the underground caverns that keep the ashes of the brave women who died in the *jauhar* when Allah-ud-din sacked the city.[1] Near by is the Palace of Padmani (the Indian Helen—but in no way like Helen in her life), looking out on its lake and tangled solitudes. The Palace is now being "repaired"—disastrously. And all about are towers and temples, each one a history in itself.

But Chitor is a place to which the mind of India goes in continual pilgrimage, and its grimness is a moving and glorious thing, infinitely more than mere horror. More terrible is the *Mahāsatī* outside Udaipur, Chitor's successor, where the later Ranas burned. Here, besides the *chhattrīs* or stone canopies, are lines of stones covered with red tinsel, the Rana's own stone, central to the whole line, being larger

[1] Probably in 1303.

CHITOR, SHOWING THE "MAHĀSATĪ"

and usually covered with silver tinsel. By counting the smaller stones you may know how many women perished with one man. It is not unusual to find a score of these stones, and I have counted over sixty in one line. Tod cites the instance of Raja Ajit Singh of Marwar (Jodhpur)—another Rajput state—with whom in 1780 sixty-four women burned:

> "No less than sixty-four females accompanied the shade of Ajit to the mansion of the sun. But this is twenty short of the number who became *satīs* when Raja Budh Singh of Bundi was drowned!"[1]

But the suttees of Rajasthan sink into insignificance beside those recorded by trustworthy authorities for some South Indian states, especially Vijayanagar during the fourteenth, fifteenth, and sixteenth centuries. Portuguese missionaries once brought the report of eleven thousand women sacrificed on the death of a South Indian Raja. This we may hope and believe was exaggeration; but we know that at Vijayanagar it was customary to burn two or even three thousand.

> "A cinder-mound near Nimbapuram, north-east of Vijayanagar, marks the scene of these appalling holocausts."[2]
>
> "This mound is composed of alternate layers of slag-like cinders and ashy earth mixed with small fragments of calcined bone."[3]

---

[1] *Annals and Antiquities of Rajasthan* (Clarendon Press, 1920, edited William Crooke), ii. 837.

[2] *Oxford History of India*, 665 n.

[3] A. H. Longhurst, *Hampi Ruins*. The identification, though probable, cannot be taken as certain.

When the Vijayanagar empire broke up, the practice was continued on a smaller scale by its chief fragment, the kingdom of Madura. Teixeira writes:

> "When I was in India, on the death of the Naique of Maduré, a country situated between that of Malauar and that of Choromandel, four hundred wives of his burned themselves along with him." [1]

This was in 1611. In 1620 a Mahommadan writer testifies:

> "The author arrived in company with his father at the city of Southern Mathura, where, after a few days, the ruler died and went to hell. The chief had seven hundred wives, and they all threw themselves at the same time into the fire." [2]

For reasons which no one has yet established, suttee seems to have increased in many parts of India between 1680 and 1830. As this period comes clearly under foreign observation, the incredible barbarity of the rite is luridly shown. The reader will find abundant evidence of this in later chapters. Nor was this wholesale immolation of the female household confined to the palaces of Central and North-Western India. In Bengal, at the beginning of the nineteenth or end of the eighteenth century, there are instances of the burning of a score or even two score women with one quite unimportant man. We read of a pyre kept alight for three days, while relays of widows

[1] Quoted in *Hobson-Jobson*, article "Suttee." [2] *Ibid.*

were fetched from a distance. The dead man was a Brahman, and these women were many of them only nominally his wives. Bengal was under the curse of kulinism, the power and prestige of the four highest Brahman clans, the *kulin* families. Many members of these made a profession of marriage, selling themselves as husbands to a great number of women, few of whom ever lived with their husband or even saw him after marriage, except when they climbed his funeral-pyre.

It was usual to burn slaves and concubines on a separate pyre from their lord's, unless the slaves were a queen's personal attendants. A lady of rank was attended on the pyre by her own female slaves.

I have mentioned the *jauhar*, the Rajput's act in utter despair, when he sent all his women to the pyre before the men rushed out on their foes. At the *jauhar* before the sack of Jaisalmer (A.D. 1295) twenty-four thousand women are said to have perished. These, of course, were the whole female population, of all ages. Equal or greater numbers must have perished in the great *jauhars* of Chitor. An early example of the rite, probably before the Rajputs had begun to enter India, occurred in a town on the Indus which Alexander the Great invested. The *jauhar* shows suttee in its noblest form.

In the Panjab and Rajasthan sometimes a mother burned on her son's pyre. This, known as *mā-satī*, "mother-suttee," was the highest kind of all, and received special honour.[1] Sometimes sisters burned with a brother. In Gujarat and Rajasthan men-slaves often attended their master's corpse as it burned. Such a slave was called *satu*, the masculine of *satī*. In 1818, together with eighteen women, eighteen men-slaves burned with the Maharaja of Jaipur, including his barber, who was sent along to shave his lord in the next world.[2]

The tenacity with which some castes and peoples of India cherished the rite was shown in 1722, when a leading merchant in the Hindu trading colony at Astrakhan, in Russia, died. The suggestion that his widow should burn was received as barbarous and permission refused, whereupon the Indian traders removed their factories and commerce from the town. Permission was then given, and the widow was burnt with due pomp and publicity.[3]

[1] H. A. Rose, *Glossary of the Tribes and Castes of the Punjab and North-West Frontier Province*, i. 201.

[2] Anne Thackeray Ritchie and Richardson Evans, *Earl Amherst* ("Rulers of India" series), 197.

[3] Peter Henry Bruce, *Memoirs* (1782), 252 ff.

## CHAPTER III

# THE FORM THAT SUTTEE TOOK

SUTTEE generally took the form of burning alive; but in the Telugu country, including Vijayanagar, it was sometimes by burial alive. The weaver caste in some parts of India—in Tippera, for example—also practised suttee by burial. Irregularly, it could be by drowning, especially when a woman had escaped from the pyre. We have an eye-witness's account of a Brahman in a boat in mid-stream at Allahabad superintending the suicide of sixteen women; but I think the *Cyclopædia of India* may be mistaken in assuming this to have been a suttee. Among the lower castes suttee was unusual, but these sometimes imitated their betters; and there are instances on record of even Mahommadans being burnt and their widows with them.

In Western India the widow "lay in a grass hut, supporting her husband's corpse with her right hand, while she set the pyre alight with a torch held in her left hand." [1] In Gujarat,

> "The pile of the Sutee is unusually large; heavy cart-wheels are placed upon it, to which her limbs are bound, or sometimes a canopy of massive logs is raised above it, to crush her by its fall. She seats herself with her husband's

[1] W. Crooke, *Things Indian*, 449.

head reclining in her lap, and, undismayed by all the paraphernalia of torment and of death, herself sets fire to the pile. It is a fatal omen to hear the sound of the Sutee's groan; as, therefore, the fire springs up from the pile there rises simultaneously with it a deafening shout of 'Victory to Umba! Victory to Runchor!' and the screaming horn and the hard-rattling drum sound their loudest until the sacrifice is consummated."[1]

In South India, in Orissa, and sometimes in Bengal, the pyre was in a pit, into which the widow jumped after the pyre was alight. In Vijayanagar the husband was burnt first, and then the widow, having changed her showy garments for coarse yellow cloth, walked three times round the pit, holding her relations' hands with one hand and a branch in the other, and then went "singing and running to the pit where the fire is,"[2] poured a pot of oil over her head, mounted some high steps, and leapt in. In North India generally, including Bengal, she climbed on the pyre and sat or lay down, with her husband's head in her lap or on her breast; the dead man's eldest son or nearest relative then lit the pile. She was by no means always left free. Especially in Bengal, she was often bound to the corpse with cords, or both bodies were fastened down with long bamboo poles curving over them like a wooden coverlet,[3] or weighted down

[1] A. K. Forbes, *Ras Mala*, 691.

[2] Ferñao Nuniz, quoted by Sewell, *A Forgotten Empire*, 40.

[3] Rammohan Ray in 1818 spoke of this custom as a recent innovation and confined to Bengal. It is significant that this constraint began to be put on widows about the time that the agitation for the abolition of suttee became strong.

with logs. Often there was a canopy, which was cut loose after the pyre was alight and smothered them.

I give two descriptions of suttee of a kind different from that best known:

> "When a captain dies, however many wives he has, they all burn themselves, and when the king dies they do the same. This is the custom throughout all the country of the heathen, except with that caste of people called Telugas, amongst whom the wives are buried alive with their husbands when they die. These go with much pleasure to the pit, inside of which are made two seats of earth, one for him and one for her, and they place each one on his own seat and cover them in little by little till they are covered up; and so the wife dies with the husband."[1] (In Vijayanagar, *circa* 1535.)

The second I condense from the account of a traveller in Bali a century ago.[2] It was the custom in that island to burn the king's corpse separately from his wives, for each of whom a separate fire-pit was prepared. The wives put off their ornaments, wounded themselves slightly in the arm and smeared their face and limbs with blood, and then mounted a scaffold from which they sprang into the pit. The scaffold was so constructed that it could be tilted towards the pit if any wife hesitated. If any wife escaped from the pyre or refused to go to it, she was killed publicly with a "krîss," or privately if she was of royal blood.

[1] Ferñao Nuniz, quoted in Sewell, *A Forgotten Empire*, 392–3 (1900 edition).

[2] *Asiatic Journal*, September–December 1830, 242.

Suttee reached its most magnificent and least squalid form among the Rajputs. I quote Sir Alfred Lyall's verse, which is substantially exact as a picture of the rite:

> Farewell! and forth must the lady ride.
>
> Her face unveiled, in rich attire,
> She strikes the stone with fingers red,
> "Farewell the palace, to the pyre
> We follow, widows of the dead!"
> And I, whose life has reached its verge,
> Bethink me of the wailing dirge
> That day my father forth was borne
> High seated, swathed in many a shawl,
> By priests who scatter flowers, and mourn;
> And the eddying smoke of the funeral.
>
> Thus did he vanish; with him went
> Seven women, by the flames set free;
> I built a stately monument
> To shrine their graven effigy:
> In front my father, godlike, stands,
> The widows kneel with folded hands;
> All yearly rites are duly paid,
> All round are planted sacred trees,
> And the ghosts are soothed by the spreading shade,
> And lulled by the strain of their obsequies.[1]

But the roots of the custom in the most primitive layers of human savagery are laid bare, beyond all possibility of hiding by those who idealize it, by the rites that accompanied it; and sometimes laid bare very crudely. The Vijayanagar *satī* flung into the fire a cloth filled with rice, also betel leaves, and then

[1] *A Rajpoot Chief of the Old School*

"her comb and mirror with which she adorned herself, saying that all these are needed to adorn herself by her husband's side."[1]

The rice and betel were for his dinner; it is possible, too, that the oil that she poured on her head was intended for his toilet, though it served the immediate purpose of shortening her own sufferings.

Suttee was particularly practised at the junction of rivers—a sacred spot in India—and in towns that were held in particular veneration, such as Benares and Gaya. Suttee shrines are usually beside water, to the west of a stream or tank, and facing east.

[1] Sewell, *A Forgotten Empire*, 41.

## CHAPTER IV

# REASONS FOR SUTTEE

DIODORUS SICULUS[1] explains the rite as an insurance against untimely death of husbands; it was adopted because wives poisoned their lords.

> "This wicked practice increasing, and many falling victims to it, and the punishment of the guilty not serving to deter others from the commission of the crime, a law was passed that wives should be burned with their deceased husbands, except such as were pregnant and had children; and that any individual who refused to comply with this aw should be compelled to remain a widow, and be for ever excluded from all rights and privileges, as guilty of impiety. This measure being adopted, it followed that the abominable disposition to which the wives were addicted was converted into an opposite feeling. For, in order to avoid that climax of disgrace, every wife being obliged to die, they not only took all possible care of their husband's safety, but emulated each other in promoting his glory and renown."[1]

Strabo heard the same story, and it was told to foreigners at intervals throughout the centuries. It may well have been one strand in the complicated and terrible selfishness that underlay the rite, that men by this means sought to ensure the most anxious servility and desire for their comfort in their homes.

Amid the intrigues of an Eastern court wives were

[1] xix. 32, 33. Quoted in J. Peggs, *India's Cries to British Humanity* (second edition, 1830), 1–2.

peculiarly susceptible as tools, as the Old Testament shows; and at some Indian courts, on the death of a Raja, a clean sweep was made of his zenana. General Hervey, in noting the burning of forty-four women with one of the Bikanir Rajas, points out that this number even included the Brahmani who provided the zenana with water. She, as of a higher caste than the women to whom she ministered, could not be considered a wife, and was simply swept away as a chattel. Hervey remarks:

> "Excessive jealousy of their female connexions, operating on the breasts of Hindoo princes, rendered those despots regardless of the common bonds of Society, and of their incumbent duty as protectors of the weaker sex, insomuch that, with a view to prevent every possibility of their widows forming subsequent attachments, they availed themselves of their arbitrary power, and under the cloak of religion introduced the practice of burning widows alive under the first impressions of sorrow or despair, immediately after the demises of their husbands." [1]

Hinduism from the first was consistent, and increasingly and inexorably diligent, in one aim—that of surrounding the male creature with every comfort and dignity. It is not always fair to blame a religion for the vices of those who practise it; but when we see people as naturally humane as those of India, certainly as endowed with the power of feeling pity as any other race, perpetuating so gross and cruel a glorification of the man, we must seek for the

[1] *Some Records of Crime*, ii. 506.

reason in the *ideas* that they were taught. Suttee was for the aggrandizement of the husband, who took with him when he died the most valuable and personal of his possessions.

> "As this awful rite was chiefly an appendage to regal and princely state, it has been considered as honourable in itself and as reflecting additional lustre on the caste and family to which the magnanimous victim belonged. In very old times it was considered an affront to the memory of the deceased, and as an evident mark of the want of that ardent devotion which a woman owes to her husband, when she showed any reluctance to accompany his body to the pile." [1]
>
> "The monuments of this noble family of the Haras are far more explicit than those of the Rathors, for every such *Satī* is sculptured on a small altar in the centre of the cenotaph: which speaks in distinct language the all-powerful motive, vanity, the principal incentive to these tremendous sacrifices." [2]

A chieftain's women were toys and dolls, just as truly as the women of the Mogul's harem. Chosen for their physical loveliness, they were moths who led a twilight existence that ended in the bewildering pomp that brought them to the flame. They were of no moment in their fluttering lives except as ornaments, and there was an ethical compulsion in the doom that sent down the dynasties whose splendour was nourished by their weakness and misery. On the score of picturesqueness, Akbar, the wary and watchful, is a poor figure beside the Rajput heroes

[1] Dubois, 172.
[2] Tod, *Annals and Antiquities of Rajasthan*, ii. 837–8

whom he overcame; and the historian marks with admiration the Sikhs whose valour exacted blood for blood from the English at Ferozeshah and Chilianwala. But it was a higher civilization that won, both with Akbar and the English. Hervey has a passage which brings out the pity of a system which looked only for prettiness and constancy in woman. He obtained the names of *satīs* who had died on the pyres of Bikanir Rajas; they were such names as:

"Ray Queen, Sun-ray, Love's Delight, Garland, Virtue Found, Echo, Soft Eye, Comfort, Moonbeam, Love-lorn, Dear Heart, Eye-play, Arbour-born, Smile, Love-bud, Glad Omen, Mist-clad, or Cloud-sprung—the last a favourite name."[1]

We may look on suttee as almost inevitable from the premiss of Hindu sociology and religion, that the husband stands to the wife in place of the Deity. Suttee, this surviving root from the darkest ages of savagery, was bound to blossom and fruit terribly, for a host of subsidiary considerations fed it. Families boasted, as they boast to-day, of their suttees, and tried to surpass rival families. Jealousy made an old man unwilling that a young and lovely woman should survive him.

"Mr. Ewer then went on to show that the sacrifice was more often designed to secure the temporal good of the survivors than the spiritual welfare of the sufferer or her husband. The son was relieved from the expense of maintaining a mother; the male relatives, reversioners in the

[1] *Some Records of Crime*, i. 242

absence of direct issue, came in at once for the estate which the widow would have held for her life; the Brahmins were paid for their services and were interested in the maintenance of their religion; and the crowd attended the show with the savage merriment exhibited by an English crowd at a boxing match or a bull-fight." [1]

This sordid greed—desire to avoid sharing a dead man's possessions with his widow—was considered by Rammohan Ray one of the causes that led to the increase of suttee in Bengal over a century ago. Hindu writers commonly blame Mahommadan lawlessness; women were unsafe, and it was best to preserve their honour by burning them when their protectors died. It is usual to blame bad Hindu customs on to Mahommadanism.

But the main sources of encouragement lay deeper than greed, deeper than even glorification of man. Hindu theology, with its doctrine of retribution pedantic in its exactitude, proved the woman left a widow a sinner whose previous life had brought upon her in this one the heaviest of all punishments in the loss of her visible God. Widowhood, then, must in rigorous justice be an experience so desolate and crammed with misery that it was better to perish in the flames that consumed the husband's corpse.

"The widow shall never exceed one meal a day, nor sleep on a bed; if she do so, her husband falls from Swarga."

"She shall eat no other than simple food, and shall daily offer the *tarpana* of *kuśa*, *tila*, and water."

---

[1] *Calcutta Review*, 1867, article "Suttee," 246.

"In *Vaisākha*, *Kārttika* and *Māgha* she shall exceed the usual duties of ablution, alms, and pilgrimage, and often use the name of God." [1]

To-day, when suttee is forbidden, the life of widows of chieftains in Central India is often too sordid for contemplation. There are fortresses packed with these wretched creatures, who exist there without ornament or amusement or pleasant food, and have no relief except squabbles among themselves and banding together to make another newly arrived consignment of widows more unhappy than themselves. A lady who knew well many of these corralled unfortunates told me that she thought it would be a reform to reintroduce suttee.

But the widow who mounted the pyre passed from the condition of a sinner to one of beatification; her dying curse or blessing had absolute power and unfettered course. After her death prayers were made to her *manes*, and those prayers were sure of fulfilment. Her dying redeemed her ancestors from hell, and she enjoyed everlasting communion with her lord. That communion was hers, even if in life he had hated her; she forced her company on him, however unlovely or uncongenial she had been to him.

"Accompanying her husband, she shall reside so long in Swarga as are the thirty-five millions of hairs on the human body.

---

[1] H. T. Colebrooke, *Miscellaneous Essays* (1873), ii. 136. The essay, *The Duties of a Faithful Hindu Widow*, was first published in 1795.

"As the snake-catcher forcibly drags the serpent from his earth, so, bearing her husband (from hell), with him she shall enjoy heavenly bliss.

"Dying with her husband, she sanctifies her maternal and paternal ancestors; and the ancestry of him to whom she gave her virginity.

"Such a wife, adoring her husband, in celestial felicity with him, greatest, most admired, with him shall enjoy the delights of heaven, while fourteen Indras reign.

"Though her husband had killed a Brahmana, broken the ties of gratitude, or murdered his friend, she expiates the crime."[1]

Everything conspired to point the widow along one path—that which led to the red glow of the funeral pyre. Once she had announced her *saṇkalpa*, or resolution (to die), no after-hesitation or terror could excuse her. Withdrawal brought ill-luck on all connected with her; die she must, however weak and miserable. About the death of a *satī* there was so much pomp and noise of applause, and about the memory of one such praise and exaltation, that often a psychological intoxication upheld her till she had passed beyond the reach of succour. It is true that widows were often drugged or narcotized, so that they became *satīs* while unaware of what they were doing. But it is not true, as many writers on the subject imagine, that such drugging was general; in Bengal it was common enough, but in Rajasthan I think it was exceptional, though perhaps not to the point of being rare. The intoxication was of the

[1] H. T. Colebrooke, *Miscellaneous Essays* (1873), ii. 135–6. Cf. the saying of Akbar quoted at the beginning of this book.

spirit, not the body; and the compulsion was terrible, being the whole tremendous, impalpable weight of familiar tradition and of expectation. If the woman were part of the enormous death-pomp of a king, going to the pyre as one in the ghostly bodyguard of a chief of Udaipur or Jodhpur or Jaipur, the splendid pageant, the women's cries of acclamation, the blare of conchs and trumpets, the elephants, the horses with their trappings, her own shining robes and vermilioned body, the fragrant gums and resin of the pyre—these things hid from her the fate awarded her. And the upward race and roar of the flames and the shouts and music of the spectators drowned any voice of agony from the fire. Our eye-witness accounts of suttee during the first three decades of last century are mostly from Bengal, and many of these speak of the extraordinary levity and callousness of the spectators. It is a puzzle for the psychologist to reconcile with this callousness that super-sensitiveness to harshness inflicted or suffering endured which commonly marks the Bengali to-day. Yet in saying this I pause, remembering the mobs who watched our own Smithfield burnings and public hangings.

CHAPTER V

# WAS SUTTEE VOLUNTARY?

I SUPPOSE that no one who has read this study so far will doubt that the *satīs* of a raja included a majority of unwilling victims. The slave-girl and concubine are chattels, and know that resistance is useless.

But it is generally believed in the West that the *satī* who died as an only wife died voluntarily, a belief which Hindus strenuously and exaltedly inculcate among themselves. We have seen that the *Oxford History* lends a modified support to this belief. But it is a belief which was not held by the Europeans who lived in Bengal during the last thirty years before the rite was suppressed; and it was not held by Rammohan Ray, who had seen his brother's wife burned, a hysterical and unhappy sacrifice. That there were many instances of a widow dying, as literature has so often depicted her, serene and uplifted beyond acknowledgment of pain, is true, though I have never been able to understand why Indian men consider this redounds to their glory. But I believe such cases were a minority.

Rajput ladies burned more willingly than those of other parts of India; this is beyond controversy.

"Rajputana women of rank seem to have been the most willing to accompany their husbands' remains to the funeral pile."[1]

"The proud Rajput women used to consider the disagreeable duty of burning themselves with their husbands a privilege attaching to their blue blood."[2]

The women being members of warrior clans whose menfolk died freely and readily in battle, the pyre seemed a smaller matter and the sacrifice a fairer thing than it did to the women of peace-loving races. Rajasthan history furnishes innumerable stories, of the most moving kind, of wives who died with their husbands; not wives only, but girls scarcely in their teens and merely betrothed to the warrior who had perished before the wedding rites could be performed. The courage of its *satīs*, no less than the desperate valour of its men, casts a sombre magnificence about the story of Chitor. It was barbarous; but when we blame a system we must remember that the men and women who suffer by living in a system have only a limited responsibility for its existence.

We may take three testimonies as to the voluntary nature of suttee during the first twenty years of last century. The first is that of C. M. Lushington, Magistrate at Trichinopoli; it brings out the fact that the worst of all compulsions is that of society pressing with a weight of training and of expectation

[1] *Cyclopædia of India*, article "Suttee."
[2] Sir Lepel Griffin, *Ranjit Singh*, 65.

on those who, as slaves were, are forced down to a sub-personal level:

"The act I apprehend is always voluntary, provided a being in a state of stupefaction and delusion can be said to possess the power of volition." [1]

The second is that of W. Ewer, Superintendent of Police, Lower Provinces, Bengal Presidency:

"It is generally supposed that a Suttee takes place with the free will and consent of the widow, and that she frequently persists in her intention to burn, in spite of the arguments and entreaties of her relations. But there are many reasons for thinking that such an event as a voluntary Suttee very rarely occurs: few widows would think of sacrificing themselves unless overpowered by force or persuasion, very little of either being sufficient to overcome the physical or mental powers of the majority of Hindoo females. A widow, who would turn with natural instinctive horror from the first hint of sharing her husband's pile, will be at length gradually brought to pronounce a reluctant consent, because, distracted with grief at the event, without one friend to advise or protect her, she is little prepared to oppose the surrounding crowd of hungry Brahmuns and interested relations, either by argument or force. . . . In this state of confusion a few hours quickly pass, and the widow is burnt before she has had time even to think on the subject. Should utter indifference for her husband, and superior sense, enable her to preserve her judgment, and to resist the arguments of those about her, it will avail her little—the people will not be disappointed of their show; and the entire population of a village will turn out to assist in dragging her to the bank of the river and in keeping her down on the pile. Under these circumstances nine out of ten widows are burnt to death." [2]

---

[1] Peggs, *India's Cries to British Humanity* (second edition, 1830), 100–1.

[2] *Ibid.*, 14–15.

This witness, who in his official duties probably had more opportunity of getting first-hand knowledge of suttees than anyone else in India, was one of those most urgent that Government should prohibit the custom.

Our third witness is the Magistrate at Bhuj, Gujarat, writing in October 1819:

> "There has been only one instance of a woman desiring to burn herself in our district, in Cutch, since 1816. In that instance I proceeded to her house, and, as she appeared firm in her resolution, I could only persuade her to delay the ceremony for a few days, promising that at the expiration of that time, if she persisted in her wish, she should meet with no hindrance. As might be expected, twenty-four hours produced a total change! Instead of the hysterical grief with which she was affected, tears came to her relief, and she declared her resolution not to burn. Her friends were very anxious that she should be dissuaded from burning."[1]

This witness brings out what we should expect to find: once the rite became rare in a district, a sentiment against it grew up, and the weight of opinion helped widows away from the pyre and not towards it.

It would be easy to find instances of *satīs* dying with courage and exaltation; and also, although Indian tradition has naturally remembered these instances alone, it would be easy to find—mostly from the testimony of European witnesses—at least as many examples of what can only be called murder of the cruellest kind. But I have chosen my eight

[1] Peggs, *India's Cries to British Humanity*, 10.

examples, irrespective of the victims' willingness or revulsion, solely to show the rite at different times and in places widely apart; all are the accounts given by eye-witnesses or obviously derived from eye-witnesses.[1]

[1] See Appendix.

## CHAPTER VI

# ATTEMPTS AT PROHIBITION: LAST YEARS OF LEGAL SUTTEE IN BRITISH INDIA

ALBUQUERQUE in 1510 prohibited suttee within the Portuguese territory of Goa. The third of the Sikh Gurus, Amar Das (1552–1574), condemned it, with how little result we shall see later. The rite aroused horror in the Mogul conquerors of India; Akbar on one occasion rode at top speed nearly a hundred miles and succeeded in saving the Raja of Jodhpur's daughter-in-law from burning against her will. He is often said to have forbidden the rite; but he could only insist that it be always voluntary, and even this restriction could not, of course, obtain in the territory of the great Rajput chieftains. His son and successor, Jahangir, in 1620 seems to have forbidden it on pain of death for those implicated in its performance; but a good deal of uncertainty hangs over these Mahommadan attempts to suppress suttee. What is certain is, the Mogul emperors strongly discountenanced it.

It is customary to say that these early efforts at suppression failed; but within the regions directly controlled by Delhi they were substantially successful, and suttee was driven into native states and outlying, semi-independent provinces such as Bengal. Charles Metcalfe,[1] who in 1829 anticipated rebellion in Bengal as a result of Lord Bentinck's prohibition, eighteen years before, when Resident at Delhi and a young man of twenty-six, had peremptorily forbidden suttee. Only once was it found necessary to resort to a show of force to prevent the rite, so completely had two centuries of Mahommadan rule eradicated the sentiment in favour of it.

Among the Marathas there seems always to have been a certain feeling against suttee which struggled with that in its favour. The Marathas have had "a bad press" with English writers, just as the Rajputs have had a conspicuously good one. As Mr. Kipling has enthusiastically reminded us:

> "The Rajput is a man and a brother, in respect that he will ride, shoot, eat pig, and drink strong waters like an Englishman. Of the pig-hunting he makes almost a religious duty, and of the wine-drinking no less." [2]

But the Maratha, though lacking in these fine qualities and often as unattractive in personal appearance as that magnificent person, the Rajput, is attractive, is a man of high intelligence, and has given his women a great deal of freedom. *Purdah*—in the West supposed to be of uniform strictness all over India—varies very greatly with the district and the race;

[1] Afterwards Lord Metcalfe. Born January 30, 1785; Resident, Delhi, 1811–1819; Governor, Jamaica, 1839; Governor-General, Canada, 1842.

[2] *Letters of Marque*, IX.

and the Maratha, as a rule, has not considered it necessary either to seclude or to burn his women. Towards the end of the eighteenth century the Maratha distaste for suttee grew, and the famous Queen Ahalya Bai, who died in 1795, discouraged it, and did her best, though in vain, to dissuade a daughter from mounting the pyre. Before the century ended two Maratha states—the Peshwa's personal dominions and, in the South of India, Tanjore—prohibited suttee. The prohibition can hardly have been entirely effective, and Tanjore relapsed later,[1] so that it became one of the few bad centres of the rite in the Indian peninsula. A third Maratha state, Savantvadi, was mentioned by the Governor of Bombay, in a letter dated May 6, 1821, as having abolished suttee ten or twelve years before.

Soon after the nineteenth century opened the Dutch administration prohibited suttee in Chinsura; and the French at Chandranagar and the Danes at Serampur, without making it an offence, suppressed it by administrative interference. Hindus resident in these towns had to take their widows into British territory and to get a British magistrate's sanction before burning them.

All these suppressions took place in small and compact districts, with the exception of the only

[1] This fact has been overlooked by the *Oxford History* and other writings that treat of suttee, and in fairness it must be mentioned, as well as the temporary prohibition.

partially successful action of the Moguls. The problem of the British Government was a much more difficult one, nor could a way be found out by the mere enquiry as to whether the rite was enjoined in the Hindu scriptures or not.

> "The practice of *satī* had been in force for so many centuries that it was an archaic and useless question for the English administration to inquire whether it was really in accordance or not with the injunctions of the early Hindu religion." [1]

Suttee was there; and in the early days of a struggling administration it was simply accepted, and there was very little notice taken of it. In February 1789 Mr. M. H. Brooks, the Collector of Shahabad, forcibly prevented a suttee and reported his action; Government approved, but told him that he must not resort to "coercive measures" or exercise of authority, but use private authority only.[2] In 1803 William Carey, the missionary, took a census [3] of suttees occurring within a circle extending thirty miles from Calcutta; the returns were necessarily inadequate, but came to four hundred and thirty-eight. Next year he placed ten reliable men at intervals throughout the same extent of country, each man being given a definite station and area of observation; they sent in monthly

[1] Demetrius C. Boulger, *Lord William Bentinck* ("Rulers of India" series), 79.

[2] The *Calcutta Review*, anonymous article "Suttee," 1867, 224.

[3] William Ward, *A View of the History, Literature, and Mythology of the Hindoos*, iii. 329 (1822 edition).

reports for six months. The number of suttees reported was less, but showed that between two and three hundred widows were burnt.[1] Carey placed these results before the Governor-General, Lord Wellesley, who was shocked and strongly inclined to prohibit the rite. Instead, in August 1805, he submitted the matter to the Supreme Court, who replied two years later, recommending that Government guide its policy by "the religious opinions and prejudices of the natives."[2] In this way Government entered on its course of vacillation and timidity, which lasted for a quarter of a century.

Meanwhile district officers from time to time found themselves in positions where the absence of definite orders concerning suttee caused embarrassment. In 1805 J. R. Elphinstone, Collector of Gaya, stopped the burning of a girl of twelve, and reported that she and her friends were "extremely grateful" for his interposition. He asked for guidance as to dealing with suttee. His question, coming with Carey's evidence, persuaded Government to get judicial opinion, as we have seen; but it was not until 1812 that his question was answered. Government were

[1] Ward. His language is loose, and may mean that the returns showed that widows were being burnt at the rate of between two and three hundred a year, or that this number were burnt in six months only.

[2] *Calcutta Review*, 1867. To this article, very much the best account of suttee ever written, I am indebted for a good deal of this summary of the events between 1805 and 1829; but most of its matter is taken from the *Parliamentary Papers* on widow-burning, 1830.

harassed by other problems—the unsuccessful siege of Bhurtpur, the growing power of Ranjit Singh, the war in Java.

In 1812 the question that had been shelved was again raised by Wauchope, an official in Bandelkhand, who merely asked what he was to do about suttee. Government and the Supreme Court looked at one another, and the Court " then exhumed " their advice of some years previously, which they had framed after referring to Hindu pundits the questions which Government in 1805 had referred to *them*. Government therefore, on December 5, 1812, having considered both the judicial and the ecclesiastical replies, observed that:

> " The practice, generally speaking, being thus recognized and encouraged by the doctrines of the Hindoo religion, it appears evident that the course which the British Government should follow according to the principle of religious toleration already noticed, is to allow the practice in those cases in which it is countenanced by their religion, and to prevent it in others in which it is, by the same authority, prohibited."

They then forbade compulsion or the use of drugs and intoxicants to tamper with the *satī's* will, and instructed magistrates to stop the rite also in the case of girls under sixteen or women who were pregnant, as in such circumstances it would be repugnant to the principles of Hindu law. The police were ordered to try to get early information of an intended suttee, and a police officer (usually a

Hindu or Mahommadan, as the few British officers could not attend the hundreds of suttees that took place) was to be present at the pyre to see that everything was in order. These instructions were unfortunate.

> "The Government and the Sudder Court [1] were, in fact, getting into a dilemma by attempting to introduce justice and law into what was, in itself, the highest kind of illegality, the most palpable injustice, and the most revolting cruelty." [2]

There can be no doubt that the new Regulations increased suttee. In 1825 the Governor of Bombay disapproved of the presence of a magistrate at the rite

> "as tending to give more dignity to the ceremony and to render the merit of the sufferer more conspicuous." [3]

In the same year C. T. Sealy, a Calcutta Judge, declared:

> "I have always been of opinion that we increased the number of Suttees by sanctioning them." [4]

In December 1818, at the end of the worst year for suttees of which we have any record, H. Oakley, Collector of Hooghly, wrote:

> "Previous to 1813 no interference on the part of the police was authorized, and widows were sacrificed legally or illegally as it might happen; but the Hindoos were then aware that the Government regarded the custom with natural horror, and would do anything short of direct prohibition

---

[1] The Supreme Court. [2] *Calcutta Review*, 1867, 235.
[3] Peggs, *India's Cries to British Humanity*, 58–9. [4] *Ibid.*, 58.

to discourage and gradually to abolish it. The case is now altered. The police officers are ordered to interfere, for the purpose of ascertaining that the ceremony is performed in conformity with the rules of the shastras, and in that event to allow its completion. This is granting the authority of Government for the burning of widows; and it can scarcely be a matter of astonishment that the number of the sacrifices should be doubled when the sanction of the ruling power is added to the recommendation of the shastra." [1]

A more cautiously worded, but not less valuable, testimony can be added:

"The Governor-General in Council is reluctantly led to express his apprehension that the greater confidence with which the people perform this rite under the sanction of Government, as implied or avowed in the circular orders already in force, combined with the excitement of religious bigotry by the continual agitation of the question, may have tended to augment, rather than diminish, the frequency of these sacrifices." [2]

In 1821 Mr. C. Smith, second judge of the Sudder Court, wrote:

"Our Government, by modifying the thing and issuing orders about it—orders which even the Government and the Sudder judges themselves do not appear clearly to comprehend—have thrown the ideas of the Hindoos upon the subject into a complete state of confusion. They know not what is allowed and what interdicted; but upon the whole they have a persuasion that our Government, whom they most erroneously suppose to be indifferent about the lives of the natives, are rather favourable to suttee than otherwise. They will then believe that we abhor the usage, when we prohibit it *in toto* by an absolute and peremptory law. They have no idea that we might not do so with the

---

[1] Peggs, *India's Cries to British Humanity*, 53

[2] *Ibid.*

most perfect safety; they conceive our power and our will to be commensurable."[1]

I think there can be no doubt that the sanction of the Government was sometimes misrepresented as an *order* that widows should burn.

The vacillation of Government was seconded by the indifference and unimaginative stupidity of the legal mind. The judicial reviews of the annual returns of suttees contain some astounding examples of pedantry. One Collector is rebuked because he had not explained the delay of a day in the case of a suttee; another is told that a washerman spectator who had pushed a widow back into the blazing pit from which she was escaping might be punished "as for a misdemeanour"; a third should have stated the widow's caste, instead of merely returning her as a Hindu; a fourth should have written "dissuaded" and not "prevented." One very bad case of suttee, the Court remarks, "bears the appearance of irregularity." Certain Collectors are

"reminded of inattention to valuable Circular Orders and of neglect to furnish information as to the condition and circumstances of the deceased."[2]

The Patna Court, on January 11, 1819, wrote:

"We have the pleasure to transmit the annual report of the number of Hindoo women who have burnt themselves

[1] *Parliamentary Papers* on widow-burning, 1830, 8.
[2] *Calcutta Review*, 1867, 237.

on the funeral piles of their husbands in the Zillah of Sarun in the year 1818." [1]

The Collector of Ghazipur used the same unexceptionable phraseology, and had

"the pleasure to forward the prescribed annual report of Suttees."

The Regulations governing suttee were not finally approved until April 1813, and were further modified on September 9, 1817:

"It was then provided with an offensive particularity that women in a state of menstruation were not to burn, nor such as had infants at the breast or under four years old, nor such as had children under seven, unless responsible persons would engage to maintain the orphans." [2]

Also *anumaraṇa* was forbidden to *brāhmanīs*, and relations of a *satī* were bound, under penalty of fine and imprisonment, to give notice to the police before the burning took place. Another order passed at the same time forbade the burying alive [3] of widows of weavers, prevalent in Tippera and other parts of East Bengal, and now considered not to be in accordance with the shastras; magistrates were to try offenders.

Against the criminal pedantry of the Courts and the timidity of Government it is fair to remember the courage of many magistrates, men of generous

[1] *Calcutta Review*, 1867, 235. See also *Parliamentary Papers*.

[2] *Calcutta Review*, 1867.

[3] The *Calcutta Review* writer makes (and repeats) the mistake of thinking that the weaver caste *burned* their widows.

instincts and humanity, who forbade suttee in their jurisdiction. And from every side the men who would have to bear the risk of rebellion if rebellion came urged abolition. So it came about that in the district round Delhi suttee had been driven out of existence, and in many wild places and bigoted towns suttee was prevented by one man's fearlessness. In some of the native states also the Resident used his influence successfully to prevent the rite. Tod, after speaking of the eighty-four *satīs* at the funeral of Raja Budh Singh of Bundi, adds with justifiable exultation:

> "Budh Singh was . . . one of the most intrepid generals of Aurangzeb; the period elapsed is about one hundred and twenty years. Mark the difference! When his descendant, my valued friend the Rao Raja Bishan Singh, died in 1821, his last commands were that none should give such a proof of their affection. He made me guardian of his infant heir. In a few days I was at Bundi, and his commands were religiously obeyed."[1]

In 1823 Sir John Malcolm wrote:

> "In the whole of Central India there have not been, as far as can be learnt, above three or four Sutties annually for the last twenty years. . . . Those shocking scenes which still occur on the death of the princes of Jeypoor, Joudpoor, and Odeypoor, to swell whose funeral honours numbers of unwilling females are forcibly thrown upon the pile, are unknown in this country."[2]

And, for one cause and another, the vigorous disapproval of such men as Tod and Malcolm being one,

[1] *Rajarthan*, ii. 838. [2] *A Memoir of Central India*, ii. 207.

suttee was at last slowly dying out, except in Rajasthan, Bengal, and the Panjab; through vast tracts of country it had practically disappeared. So completely had it faded out of the tradition of the district round Delhi and much of what later became the United Provinces, that even in the mighty incandescence of Hindu passion and sentiment in the Mutiny of 1857 we do not hear of suttees. We should have heard of them abundantly if Rajasthan or Bengal had been among our enemies. In those parts of (what later became) the United Provinces where suttee existed a hundred and twenty years ago it was in infinitely less vogue than in Bengal. Maratha sentiment, after a temporary yielding, was gathering against the rite. Even at Poona, between 1800 and 1810, its occurrence had dropped to about a dozen cases annually "on the average of as many years."[1] Dubois, in 1816, wrote that suttee was "more rare in the peninsula than in the northern parts of India"[2]; and Elphinstone, whose impressions were formed about the same time, though published twenty-three years later, states that it never occurred to the south of the river Krishna[3]—a statement not true, though the rite was rare in the south and yearly growing rarer. In the Bombay and Madras Presidencies, during the years 1815 to 1820, the average number

[1] Edward Moor, *Hindu Pantheon* (edited W. O. Simpson, 1864), 318.

[2] Edited Pope, 172.

[3] *History*, 209 (1874 edition).

of annual suttees was well below fifty. In Madras it was less common in the centre, and in the west and south unknown, except in Tanjore and one estate in Kanara.[1] Tanjore, now the worst district, had twenty-four cases in eighteen months (*circa* 1816). About the same time the Judge of South Malabar spoke of it as entirely absent; there had been two attempts to perform it, but the people themselves had opposed them, and the funeral parties had been compelled to take their widows to Coimbatore to burn.

> "Since that time nothing of the kind has been attempted, nor would the natives quietly permit it on the soil of Malabar."[2]

We must now return to the effect of the 1813 Regulations in Bengal. There are no returns for 1814, owing to the delay in finally sanctioning the orders originally made out in December 1812. But the first four years for which returns were made give the following result in the districts subordinate to the Presidency of Bengal:

1815. 378 suttees were officially reported.
1816. 442 suttees were officially reported.
1817. 707 suttees were officially reported.
1818. 839 suttees were officially reported.

In 1818, the year when the pyres blazed most fiercely, Rammohan Ray began to publish his pamphlets against the rite, action which aroused such anger that for a while his life was in danger. But

[1] *Calcutta Review*, 1867, 233 [2] *Ibid.*

he awakened a conscience in his own countrymen, which presently found expression in protests in native newspapers; and the number of suttees never reached this height again. The awful record of 1818 disquieted many officials exceedingly; and in England indignation began to gather, which ultimately put upon the Indian Government a pressure that they could not withstand. On June 17, 1823, the Court of Directors, answering a letter of the Supreme Court, Calcutta, of October 1, 1820, pointed out the apparent tendency of the rules and of official interference to increase suttee; they added that many considered it not a religious rite at all, and they invited the Indian Government to take the question up seriously, promising their hearty co-operation. Lord Amherst, the Governor-General, wrote back despairingly on December 3, 1824:

> "Were we to be guided by the sentiments which we happen to know exist generally among the higher classes of natives at the place most favourable for ascertaining their real sentiments, we mean at the Presidency, we should, indeed, despair of ever seeing the suppression of the practice."

But on March 18, 1827, we find him soothing himself in his policy of inactivity thus:

> "But after all, I must frankly confess, though at the risk of being considered insensible to the enormity of the evil, that I am inclined to recommend our trusting to the progress now making in the diffusion of knowledge amongst the natives for the gradual suppression of this detestable superstition. I cannot believe it possible that the burning or burying alive of widows will long survive the advancement

which every year brings with it in useful and rational learning."

It is interesting to analyse the figures for the first four years of returns. Of the total (2,366), 1,485 suttees occurred in the Calcutta Division; 343 in Benares, then, as now, the metropolis of Hindu bigotry, but in this matter far behind Calcutta, where often the presence of European magistrates and sometimes of horrified English ladies kindled the crowds to an intoxication of delight; 155 in the densely populated but strongly Mahommadan Division of Dacca; 155 in Patna,[1] where the population was perhaps thinnest but Hindu sentiment was, and is, strong; 105 in the Murshidabad Division, another centre of Mahommadan influence; 60 in Bareilly.

There was considerable carelessness as to keeping within even the wide latitude allowed by the Directions. Between 1815 and 1820 twenty-two widows of sixteen were burned, and twenty-four under that age, three being children eight years old. In 1818 forty-nine widows were under twenty, a hundred and twenty-two between twenty and thirty, eight were returned as over ninety, and two as over a hundred. It was found, too, that in *anumaraṇa* there was sometimes a long delay after the husband's death—intervals of five, ten, or even fifteen years were reported. It is hard to suppose that in these cases

[1] Suttee has occurred in this district several times in the present century.

affection, after so long a space in which memory was blurring, awakened to such a pitch of resolution; but it is easy to see how the wearing misery of a widow's lot might hound her into a belated martyrdom to escape from life.

The Supreme Court, though refusing to recommend the prohibition of suttee, did not allow it to take place within their immediate jurisdiction; Calcutta suttees had to take place in the suburbs. The writer of the article in the *Calcutta Review* of 1867, after observing that in 1819 fifty-two widows were returned as having been burnt in the suburbs, remarks:

> "It is, therefore, quite clear that any respectable British householder living at Cossipore, Ballygunge, Alipore, or Garden Reach, and driving into Town for his daily work, or any resident within the ditch, might, if they desired it, reckon on being horrified by a ceremony of this kind, on an average, once a week." [1]

After 1818 the number of suttees dropped considerably, though never as low as its pre-Regulation level:

SUTTEES IN THE BENGAL PRESIDENCY.

| Year | Number |
|---|---|
| 1819 .. .. | 650 |
| 1820 .. .. | 598 |
| 1821 .. .. | 653 |
| 1822 .. .. | 583 |
| 1823 .. .. | 575 |
| 1824 .. .. | 572 |
| 1825 .. .. | 639 |
| 1826 .. .. | 518 |
| 1827 .. .. | — |
| 1828 .. .. | 463 |

[1] *Calcutta Review*, 1867, 232.

I cannot find that any returns were made for either 1827 or 1829. The increased number of 1825 was ascribed to an outbreak of cholera, in which over twenty thousand died; the increase led to renewed protest against the rite.

It is clear to me, from consideration of the districts where suttee prevailed most and from such knowledge of India and of Hinduism as I have, that the custom was one which Vaishnavism tended to discourage, while Saktism enormously increased it, in spite of the fact that the *Tantras* forbade it. In the strongly Vaishnava district of Vishnupur, a kingdom which existed from about A.D. 600 to the end of the eighteenth century, and was, and is, fervently Hindu, with hardly a Christian in it and few Mahommadans, and those uninfluential, there are traditions of suttee, but they are vague. The only *definite* one that I traced during many years of familiarity with the place was the story that supplied the germ-thought of my drama "The Clouded Mirror."[1] I was told of a suttee in the neighbouring village of Maliara about a century ago, and I heard occasionally of others dimly remembered elsewhere, and I know places where a suttee must have been the original event that has been twisted into a different tale. When we remember that this district is scarcely a hundred miles from Calcutta, it is strange that it should be without suttee-stones, even at the *sangam*

[1] See *Three Eastern Plays*.

(junction) of rivers. There are suttee-stones, but the people have forgotten what they are and explain them otherwise. But the Jungle Mahals, in which the district lay, returned comparatively few suttees in the awful records of a century ago; and Midnapur, which lies still nearer to Calcutta, returned still fewer. I am aware that the rite must have occurred oftener than men now recall, and in the country districts the people have kept a name for a *satī—āgunkhākī*, "one who has eaten fire." Where the word *satī* is misunderstood or an answer refused, this less sacred word will enlighten at once and bring out such records as the village memory has kept. But the rite was rare where Vaishnava influence reigned; the *satīs* died most numerously in Calcutta, its suburbs and the towns that cling to its outskirts, and in Nadiya, the metropolis of Bengali history and Hindu learning and enthusiasm. Calcutta Hinduism, though cherishing a literary and sentimental fondness for Vaishnava poetry, in its deeper and fiercer currents is Sakta, and worships the terrible Goddess Kali, as does Rajasthan. The great Vaishnava devotee of Rajasthan, the Queen Mira Bai, had to leave her home and family and live and die in exile. She was a Vaishnava from childhood, and for her religion was persecuted and driven from Chitor.

## CHAPTER VII

# PROHIBITION IN BRITISH INDIA

LORD WILLIAM CAVENDISH-BENTINCK had served as Governor of Madras twenty-two years before he was appointed Governor-General of India in 1827; but he had never seen a suttee-stone, and he brought to the question of continuing or prohibiting the rite a mind fresh and independent. A passage in Sleeman's *Rambles and Recollections* is of such interest that I transcribe it a little more fully than is strictly relevant to my purpose:

"When I passed this place on horseback with Lord Bentinck, he asked me what these tombs were, for he had never seen any of the kind before. When I told him what they were, he said not a word; but he must have felt a proud consciousness of the debt of gratitude which India owes to the statesman who had the courage to put a stop to this great evil, in spite of all the fearful obstacles which bigotry and prejudice opposed to the measure. The seven European functionaries in charge of the seven districts of the newly acquired territories were requested, during the administration of Lord Amherst in 1826, to state whether the burning of widows could or should be prohibited; and I believe every one of them declared *that it should not*. And yet, when it was put a stop to only a few years after by Lord William, not a complaint or murmur was heard. The replies to the Governor-General's inquiries were, I believe, throughout India, for the most part, opposed to the measure." [1]

[1] *Rambles*, i. 133–4 (1893 edition).

Sleeman is speaking from hearsay, and it could be shown that he was mistaken, except in what he says of "the seven European functionaries in charge of the seven districts of the newly acquired territories," which were districts that he knew well at first hand. These districts were all in Central India abutting on Rajputana, where the pro-suttee feeling was strongest, and the few Europeans were in charge of

> "New-caught, savage peoples,
> Half-devil and half-child."

Even so, Vincent Smith's comment is fair and true:

> "The tenor of the replies given to Lord Amherst's queries shows how far the process of Hinduizing had advanced among the European officials of the Company." [1]

But it had not advanced so far among the officials in parts of India that had been longest under British rule; and Peggs collects some forty statements made by East India Company servants in the dozen years preceding the abolition that suttee could be abolished without any danger, and ought to be abolished without delay.

Lord Bentinck took over in July 1828, and he did not act without the most careful preliminary investigation and consultation of officials and pundits. But he was resolute to act upon a purpose with which his predecessors had only played—Lord Wellesley

[1] *Rambles* (Sleeman), i. 134 (1893 edition).

having been dissuaded by the supposed danger in the army, and Hastings and Amherst having been driven into perplexed and unhappy courses of allowing suttee under legal sanction. Many predicted rebellion if the custom were prohibited; the native army especially was alleged to be bigoted in its adherence to the rite. But Bentinck ascertained that suttee was very rare indeed in our native army, which is not strange, seeing that, except for about a thousand men in the artillery, the army was not recruited from Bengal at all, but from the up-country where Moslem rulers had through two hundred years discouraged suttee. Of forty-nine British military officers asked for their opinion, a majority advocated abolition, some with more or less hesitation, but over twenty without any; only five were in favour of leaving the practice alone. The Governor-General's long Minute on suttee is as masterly in its summary of the opposition and reasons for opposition and of the overwhelming argument in favour of abolition as it is honourable to himself. And there proved to be no disturbance, even when the appeal of many religious and influential Bengalis was rejected by the Privy Council in 1832.

The abolition of suttee, so far from being, like the abolition of slavery, an example of our greatness as a nation and an empire, is an example of our timidity. In this instance we have taken to ourselves praise beyond our desert. The credit is almost entirely personal, and it is Bentinck's. Many who hated the rite would have withdrawn from prohibition at the last moment. Mr. Coomaraswamy coolly remarks that

> "It was prohibited by law in 1829 on the initiative of Raja Rammohun Roy." [1]

Rammohan Ray was a valiant fighter against suttee, but he thought the prohibition an inexpedient measure, as did Sir Charles Metcalfe, who had forbidden suttee at Delhi more than seventeen years previously.

On Sunday morning, December 5, 1829, a document was brought to the Rev. William Carey, with the Governor-General's request that he would translate it.

> "It was nothing less than the famous Edict abolishing *satī* throughout British dominions in India! Springing to his feet and throwing off his black coat, he cried, 'No church for me to-day!' . . . 'If I delay an hour to translate and publish this, many a widow's life may be sacrificed,' he said. By evening the task was finished." [2]

Regulation XVII of 1829 made the burning or burying alive of widows culpable homicide, punishable with fine or (and) imprisonment. When compulsion or the use of drugs deprived the *satī* of free will, the offence might be punished with death as murder. It came into immediate operation in Bengal, and was adopted in Madras and Bombay six months later. It was adopted with these modifications in Bombay:

[1] *The Dance of Siva*, 92.
[2] F. Deaville Walker *William Carey*, 310.

that the offence was murder if the widow were under eighteen, and an extreme limit of ten years' imprisonment was set for suttee that was not murder. These laws lasted until 1860, when an Act made assistance in suttee punishable as abetment of suicide.

The opposition of the religious and learned babus of Calcutta was fierce, as had been predicted; but it was ordained that it should take a comic form, that the long-drawn-out tragedy might reveal its bitter absurdity in the end. On January 14, 1830, the Governor-General received a deputation of Bengali gentlemen who objected to their loss of the right to show their religious convictions in the old ferocious way. The Governor-General later in the day replied, inflexible in his resolution to suppress suttee, and pointing out that the protestants had

"an appeal to the King in Council, which the Governor-General shall be most happy to forward."

A committee was formed, and over eight hundred signatures obtained to an appeal to the Privy Council to restore suttee. At an enthusiastic meeting Mr. Francis Bathie was given full power of attorney and appointed to take the Petition to England; it was voted that he should have all the funds he needed, and he assured them that he was certain of success. The ship in which he first sailed had an accident with a cable chain and sprang a bad leak; it was hastily run ashore. Mr. Bathie wrote to his patrons:

"Such accidents are generally attended with the loss of life; but from my being the bearer of the suttee petition, God has saved all who were with me." [1]

He further pointed out that the delay gave a chance for suttee enthusiasts who lived at a distance from Calcutta and had been unable to sign the Petition to send their signatures in now. The *Chandrikā*, the journal that expressed the views of the orthodox Hindu community, was very impressed with the friendly attitude shown by Providence in the affair. But a correspondent in the *India Gazette* was impious enough to ascribe the accident to the very fact that such a petition was on board; and the *Kaumudī*, the journal of the anti-suttee party among the Hindus, observed:

"The petition sent to England, to procure the restoration of the burning of women, so humanely abolished by the Governor-General, has been brought back, by force of the virtuous merit of the whole female sex of our country, for the ship which bore it was very nearly carried to the bottom."

Mr. Bathie ultimately reached England; and Mr. Lushington argued before the Privy Council on behalf of the religious rites which Lord Bentinck had stopped, contrary to the engagement of the Government not to interfere with liberty of conscience. But Rammohan Ray, who was in England, obtained access to members of Parliament and was consulted

[1] Was the good man by any chance remembering Acts xxvii. 23–24?

by the Privy Council, and with all the emphasis and power of his amazing intellect and personality begged them to support the action which he had thought premature but believed to be altogether righteous. The Privy Council in 1832 rejected the appeal of the pro-suttee party; and Rammohan Ray procured a petition from progressive and humane Hindus thanking Lord Bentinck for what he had done. His services were a fitting crown to the brave life of the great Indian. Next year he died, and his body lies in an English churchyard.

## CHAPTER VIII

## THE SUPPRESSION OF SUTTEE IN NATIVE STATES

WITH Lord Bentinck's prohibition of suttee a new social conscience came to the Indian Government, and the next thirty years saw them warring against female infanticide, thuggee, human sacrifice, slavery, suttee, and all forms of indigenous barbarity. The Western reader who troubles about India at all generally assumes that the 1829 and 1830 Regulations were the end of suttee everywhere, and there is no historian who indicates how terribly it was still practised throughout a vast tract of territory. It took many years to disappear, and it will be instructive to watch the Paramount Power stamping it out in one area after another and reducing the extent within which it was legal.

After the abolition in British India, the rite existed in Northern and Western India, between the Narbada and the Indus, and from the United Provinces to Sind. Within this tract it had three main strongholds: (1) the states on the northern border of Bombay Presidency—those clustering along the Narbada, and Baroda and the Kathiawar states; (2) Rajputana; (3) the Sikh empire and the states lying between it and British India, dependent on one of these two powerful neighbours or precariously independent. Suttee existed also in Nepal, which was outside British influence, and in one or two outlying wilds such as Assam and Orissa.

As suttee was a matter of internal polity, Residents at native courts could only express *unofficially* the abhorrence of their own Government when it occurred; it was not until that masterful man Lord Dalhousie became Governor-General that interference took a peremptory form. Nevertheless, the British Government let slip no chance that territorial changes or the revision of treaties afforded of securing promises to prohibit the rite. It seems to me beyond controversy that Indian opinion and Indian princes would have allowed suttee, and a host of horrors besides, to continue indefinitely but for this alien vigour in the land.

The first chance to extend the area of abolition came on March 2, 1833, when a Raja was being installed in Assam. He was made to promise

> "to abstain from the practice of the former Rajahs of Assam, as to cutting off ears and noses, extracting eyes, or otherwise mutilating or torturing, and that he will not inflict cruel punishment in his territory for slight faults"[1];

and also to prohibit suttee.

[1] C. U. Aitchison, *Treaties, Engagements, and Sunnuds* (1876 edition), i. 172.

## Suttee in Western India.

I have said that the attitude of the British Government towards the rite in native states was strictly correct. But progress was sometimes accelerated by an individual officer going beyond his duty of registering protest. One such instance, in 1835, started the Bombay Government on a course of vigorous and persistent pressure that within five years cleared suttee out of the states on their borders.

I must go back to an event of 1833. The state of Idar, a Rajput state close to the Bombay Presidency, from ancient times had had a barbaric pre-eminence for its *satīs*.

> "Idar is surrounded by a brick wall in fair preservation, through which a road passes by a stone gateway, marked with many red hands each recording a victim to the rite of *satī*." [1]

On September 5, 1833, before a vast crowd, a ceremonial took place that shocked British opinion in India: seven queens, two concubines (of different caste from their dead master), four female slaves, and a personal manservant were burnt with the body of the Raja of Idar. Before the pyres were lit the eldest rani, addressing the crowd, said that she had always intended to burn with her lord, and that no appeal could have turned her from her purpose; but she thought it strange that she had heard no single

[1] *Imperial Gazetteer of India*, vol. xiii.

word of compassion or dissuasion. She bade those who were now sweeping her master's household out of their way to obtain the widows' inheritance to go and live on the plunder they were getting. The *Karbaris* (officers) followed the funeral with an extensive pillage of the Raja's personal property.

The incident[1] has an interest beyond its pathos; it shows what from now on is increasingly manifest—that the women of royal households in native India were changing in their attitude towards suttee, now that their sisters in British India were no longer allowed to burn.

Two years later the Raja of the neighbouring principality of Ahmadnagar died. His state had formerly been part of Idar state, as it is to-day, and it shared the same ferocious traditions. The British Agent, Mr. Erskine, who was in charge of both states, was now in the neighbourhood of Ahmadnagar. Determined to prevent a repetition of the Idar suttee, he moved on the town with a force of three hundred men. All day long, on February 8th, the deceased Raja's sons pleaded with him not to interfere with their customs; they used the delay to push on their desperate measures for the sacrifice of the ranis. Finding Erskine resolute, they secretly summoned warriors from the Bhils and other turbulent tribes, and the British Agent became aware that men armed with spears and matchlocks were pouring into the

[1] My authority is the *Bombay Courier*, September 28, 1834.

fort. He advanced upon it, but was fired on, some of his men being wounded; he fell back, sent for artillery, and waited. About two o'clock in the morning women's screams were heard and the red glow of a pyre was seen on the darkness. During the night part of the fort wall had been broken down, and the widows, five in number, dragged to the river-bed and burnt. It was too late to rescue them. That the *satīs* had been unwilling ones was clear. A woman's arm, hacked off by an axe or sword, lay in the ashes. The princes fled, but subsequently surrendered to Erskine.[1]

Erskine's action had been beyond his legal powers; but his Government supported him against cruelty and insolence so great. In a lengthy memorandum dated February 18, 1836, the new Ahmadnagar ruler provided a scapegoat and confessed:

"My minister Mahadjee Soobhavut is guilty in the affair of the suttee; I will not give him shelter within my territory."

He promised also:

"From this time forward neither I nor my children nor my posterity will perform the ceremony of suttee."[2]

In 1840 the Bombay Government clinched matters

[1] I rely on the *Bombay Courier* and the *Imperial Gazetteer of India* (1909), ii. 443. The *Gazetteer* gives the number of *satīs* as three. Official documents often omit to count slaves or concubines, and the *Courier* account is within a few months of the event, more than seventy years earlier than the *Gazetteer*.

[2] *Treaties, Engagements, and Sunnuds*, iv. 76.

by a proclamation that any village or district in the Ahmadnagar territory where suttee occurred would be placed under attachment.

For many years after the prohibition of suttee in their own jurisdiction the Bombay Government was annoyed by the asylum given to it by neighbouring states. British subjects, refused permission to burn in Bombay, were taken across the border and burnt in states where the law against suttee did not obtain. The chief of the little island known as Angria's Kolaba, about twenty miles from Bombay, and Pratap Singh, the Raja of Satara, were particular offenders. Pratap Singh, a capable ruler but unfriendly, ignored the protests of the British representative, and suttee became very common in Satara. The Bombay Government, sensitive under the loss of prestige that resulted when their laws were flouted, although beyond their borders, began to follow up cases of the burning of their own subjects. On January 3, 1838, a peccant chieftain, the Nawab of Junagarh, was compelled to make confession and promise to prohibit the rite altogether, a course that the British Government was bound to force upon native states once it insisted that its own subjects were not to be burnt:

"After compliments.—The cause of writing to you is this. A certain Bhattianee having arrived from Bombay and committed suttee at Pragrye, and the Sircar having issued orders preventive of such a practice, a mohsul is upon me in order to make me answerable; and the particulars of the subject (the suttee) having been reported to Government, and it having been considered as a first instance of the kind, for which reason I have been pardoned, I give this writing to the effect that from henceforward such measures in the talooka will be taken so that no person will be allowed to become suttee in future. But if such should hereafter occur, I am responsible to any extent the Sircar may pronounce against me." [1]

At the same time another chief in the Kathiawar Agency, the Sidi of Jafirabad, was made to enter into the same agreement. Then, in September 1839, the Satara Raja was deposed. His offence was that he had intrigued with the Portuguese and some native princes against the British; but he had been a nuisance in other ways, his patronage of suttee being one. His brother became Raja, and at his accession of his own free will abolished the rite, later proving his good faith by preventing a woman from being burnt.

Next year, 1840, in the absence of direct heirs, Angria's Kolaba "lapsed" to the British Raj. The same year the Government wrote sharply to the foremost prince in the Bombay Presidency, the Gaekwar of Baroda, and cleansed that side of India from legal suttee by promises wrung from the leading chiefs of Rewa Kanta, the territory lying along the Mahi—the Raja of Chota Udaipur, the Maharanas of Lunawara and Rajpipla, the Rana of Sonth, and the Thakurs of Bhadurwah, Wankanir, and Deogarh

[1] *Treaties, Engagements, and Sunnuds*, iv. 145

Barria. The context of the Government's demand is made clear by the Despatch of Mr. A. Remington, Officiating First Political Commissioner and Resident at Baroda:

(Date, April 3, 1840.) "Under instructions received from the Resident of Baroda, conveyed to me in his letter dated 11th March, 1840, I write to inform you that it having come to the notice of that officer that a British subject born in Rutnagherry, but residing at Baroda, died, and his widow immolated herself in observance of the rite of suttee, which the Guikwar government took no measures to prevent, the Political Commissioner addressed a note to His Highness deprecating the occurrence, and suggesting that, as the British Government had, after full consideration, abolished the rite of suttee in its own territory, His Highness should introduce a similar arrangement within his own, to which His Highness replied that, according to the request of the Resident, he would cause proper arrangement to be made; and this concurrence being communicated to Government, it was pleased to declare that no act could have been performed more acceptable to it than the abolition of suttee. I beg to state that it appears to me advisable you should take measures to prohibit the practice in your own State, in respect of which, as the British Government are most intent on the speedy abolition of this rite, you will have the goodness, after full consideration of the above, to favour me with a reply." [1]

All agreed to suppress suttee.

On the other side of India, Government had embarked on the task of extirpating the horrible "meriah" human sacrifices of the Orissa highlands. Progress was slow, and success was not attained till some years later. In the meantime fifteen tributary

[1] *Treaties, Engagements, and Sunnuds*, iv. 251.

rajas, zemindars, and mehals of Orissa were made to promise, by a statement dated April 14, 1842, to abolish suttee, adding:

> "Further, if on the demise of a Rajah any of his Ranees should actually desire to become 'suttees,' and should disregard our prohibition, we will restrain them from becoming 'suttees,' and make a report of the circumstance to the Superintendent, and conform to such orders as we may receive from him. Without the Superintendent's orders (or permission) we will not allow any person to become a suttee. And we engage unhesitatingly to submit ourselves to any penal orders which the Superintendent of the Tributary Mehals may issue, if we shall act in any way contrary to the engagements of this Recognizance." [1]

### Suttee among the Sikhs.

We have seen the British Government dealing with native governments prejudiced in favour of suttee and unable to see why, if a woman had sufficient virtue to wish to die with her husband's corpse, she should not be allowed to do so. But they were states with little power and of secondary rank, and had no choice but to accept the demands of their overlord. Their compliance left intact the real strongholds of suttee, the powerful Sikh confederacy and the stubborn and bigoted Rajput principalities. The former was destined to fight two fierce wars with the British, and at Chilianwala to achieve a drawn battle which is merely a sentence in our histories, but with Halighat (the great Rajput defeat, a glorious one,

[1] *Treaties, Engagements, and Sunnuds*, i. 120.

by the Moguls in 1576) is the most cherished martial memory of secret India.

Among the Sikhs

"the suttee murders were atrocious. Four ladies burned with Ranjit Singh; one, against her will, with Kharak Singh; two with Nao Nihal Singh; 310 (10 wives and 300 unmarried ladies of his zenana) were sacrificed at the obsequies of Raja Suchet Singh; in September 1845 four wives of Jawahir Singh were forced on the pyre by the soldiery; and, after Sobraon, the widow of Sardar Shan Singh burnt voluntarily."[1]

But neither Vincent Smith, in this inaccurate summary, nor the many writers who have quoted it, have indicated how incredibly atrocious the suttees of the last years of Sikh independence were. Contemporary British opinion in India was appalled by the obsequies of Ranjit Singh, "the Lion of the Panjab," in July 1839; but Vigne, who gives the number of *satīs* wrongly, speaks justly when he says:

"Seven women only were burned with the body of Ranjit Singh—a very small number, considering his rank; but it was no doubt deemed expedient to show some respect to European prejudices."[2]

We have two accounts of the scene by European eye-witnesses[3]; the accounts contradict each other in minor details, but prove the general inaccuracy of Thorburn's graphic and brilliant description.[4] The

[1] *Oxford History*, 689–690 n.

[2] *Travels in Kashmir, Ladak, Iskardo* (1842), 86.

[3] John Martin Honigberger, the Court Physician at Lahore, and the adventurer Lieutenant-Colonel Henry Steinbach.

[4] *The Punjab in Peace and War*, 20–21.

four queens came first, walking barefooted from the palace to the body, which was fastened to a wooden board; before each of them a man walked backward, holding a mirror in which the lady could watch her countenance and detect the first glimmer of terror or shrinking. Three had already given their jewels away; the fourth was scattering gifts from a tray carried beside her by a man attendant. All four were in plain silk, without any ornaments. The chief queen, Rani Kundan, placed the hands of the minister and of the new Maharaja and his son on the corpse's breast, and made them swear to be faithful to the Khalsa and to one another, or incur a *satī's* curse. The four ranis were then taken up in gorgeous palanquins, before which their mirror and a gilt parasol, the symbol of their rank, were carried. They were borne between a long double line of infantry as down a street; behind them walked seven slave-girls, also barefooted and plainly clad. The board to which the body of their master was fastened was placed on a brilliantly decorated bier, shaped like a ship, with flags and silken sails embroidered with gold and silver. The pyre was about six feet high, and its surface scattered with cotton-seeds and other inflammable stuffs. The queens, Steinbach tells us, were excited and exultant; the slaves, some of whom seemed only fourteen or fifteen years old, resigned.[1]

[1] *The Punjaub* (1846). Psychologically, his account is the more detached and valuable, but Honigberger's contains the fuller details.

At the pyre there was an hour's prayer, following on the drums and dirges of the procession; and then the state ministers mounted the pyre by a ladder and set the corpse upon it. They descended, and the queens and slaves went up, Raja Dhyan Singh, the chief minister, being particularly officious in helping them. The ranis seated themselves at the head of their master, the slaves at the feet; and all sat cowering and silent, the ranis ignoring Dhyan Singh's request that they would pray for the new Maharaja's prosperity. A thick mat of reeds was put over all the bodies and drenched in oil; then the pile was lit at the four corners and the flames shot up. The whole took two days to burn.

The heroism and beauty of the victims threw their fate into lurid relief, though the scene in itself was merely repetition of countless similar scenes that India has witnessed through the ages. One of the women was the famous "Lotus," a dancing-girl whose loveliness made a great impression on the British Mission at Ranjit Singh's court the previous year:

> "His four wives, all very handsome, burnt themselves with his body, as did five of his Cachmerian slave-girls, one of whom, who was called the Lotus or Lily, I often saw last year in my first visit to Lahore." [1]

The Hon. Emily Eden, in her charming letters, wrote:

> "Those poor dear ranees, whom we visited and thought so beautiful and so merry have actually burnt themselves.

---

[1] Hon. W. Osborne, *The Court and Camp of Runjeet Singh* (letter dated July 12, 1839).

. . . The death of those poor women is so melancholy; they were such gay young creatures, and they died with the most obstinate courage." [1]

Her letter of the previous day (July 2, 1839), when the sacrifice was merely reported as in prospect, contained the cynicism:

"I begin to think that the 'hundred wife system' is better than the mere one wife rule; they are more attached and faithful." [2]

The British Government instructed Mr. Clerk, their representative at Lahore, to convey their horror. But the six years of murder, intrigue, and anarchy that followed Ranjit Singh's death—years so terrible in their indiscriminate butchery that it is hard to parallel them in recent history anywhere—found the Sikhs very careless of what the British Government thought, especially of what it thought "unofficially." With Ranjit Singh's death the last shreds of regard were quickly swept away. Sixteen months later the funeral obsequies of his successor were held:

"On the funeral pile of his son, Maharaja Kharak Singh, one of his *chadar dalna* [3] wives, a beautiful woman named Isar Kour, was burnt. She was unwilling to be a *satī*, and it is said that she was forced to burn by the minister Raja Dhyan Singh." [4]

---

[1] *Up the Country* (1867), 310. [2] *Ibid.*, 309.

[3] "Throwing the sheet"—a Sikh form of marriage with the brother of a deceased husband.

[4] Sir Lepel Griffin, *Ranjit Singh* ("Rulers of India" series), 65.

Dhyan Singh had superintended the scene at Ranjit Singh's pyre, and had consummated his action by the hypocrisy of pretending to wish to be burnt with his master himself, pushing himself forward with loud cries and being "forced" back.

Kharak Singh had been deposed by his son and his favourites slaughtered on October 8, 1839; he died a year later, on November 5, 1840, probably by poison. Two ranis and eleven slave-girls were burnt with him. His son, Maharaja Nao Nihal Singh, a boy of nineteen, left the pyre while his father's body was still burning, and was crushed by the falling of an archway on his way home, dying before midnight. Two wives burned with him. His successor, Shere Singh, was assassinated September 15, 1843, and burned with "the usual suttee rites,"[1] no writer troubling to specify their extent. The minister, Dhyan Singh, was murdered the same day. His widow and slave-girls, designated for his pile,

> "were kept waiting before the troops to inspire them with revenge, and the spectacle of their melancholy and dismal figures increased their fury a hundredfold."[2]

After her stepson, Hira Singh, had brought the head of her husband's slayer and laid it at her feet, the widow and her thirteen slave-girls mounted the pyre, first assuring Hira Singh that she would take a good

[1] Steinbach, 38.

[2] Syad Muhammad Latif, *History of the Panjab*, 517. See also Major S. Carmichael Smyth, *History of the Reigning Family of Lahore* (1847), 85–6.

report of him to his father. A slave-girl aged ten, spared as too young, begged to be included, and was allowed to join the other *satīs* before the pile was lit.

Next year occurred the most horrible of all these Sikh suttees. Raja Suchet Singh, famous for his personal beauty and gallant bearing, attempted the throne, but was slain on March 27, 1844, after a fight in which he and his companions showed wonderful prowess. It was followed by suttees suitable to the rank and valour of the slain. Eleven women died with Kishari Singh, five with Basanta Singh, eleven with Nihal Singh [1]; but with Suchet Singh, the leader, ten wives and three hundred concubines were burnt.

> "some at Lahore, a hundred and fifty at Ramnagar, where his head was brought, and the others at Jammu or their own homes." [2]

These suttees were scattered over a wide area and the time was one of utter confusion, so that the case does not seem to have attracted the attention of British India till afterwards, nor the appalling scale of the sacrifice to have been known till Frederic Drew in his travels learnt it. The evidence, which comes from many sources, is so contradictory that neither the *Oxford History's* statement nor that of Vincent Smith's authority, Sir Lepel Griffin, can be

[1] W. L. M'Gregor, *The History of the Sikhs* (1846), ii. 29. He gives forty-five as the number of suttees with Suchet Singh.

[2] Griffin, *Ranjit Singh*, 65.

taken as without exaggeration. But it is certain that the *satīs* were very many, and the funeral ceremonies burnt themselves into the Sikh memory and are still talked of.

On December 21, 1844, Suchet Singh's conqueror, Hira Singh, son of Dhyan Singh, was killed, and burned with twenty-four[1] *satīs* at Parmandal, near Jammu. His funeral was described to Drew by an eye-witness:

> "There was a large square stage made, built up of faggots, with a rough roof raised over it; between the faggots *ghi*, that is clarified butter, was placed, to increase the violence of the flames. The women, twenty-two in number, were seated on the platform; the wood was fired, and the burning was finished without a scream or a voice being heard from them."[2]

Less than a year later, Hira Singh's conqueror, Jawahir Singh, whom Sir Lepel Griffin calls "debauched and infamous"[3]—though it is hard to see how any one of the Sikh leaders in these years could claim the pre-eminence in turpitude that such epithets imply—was executed by the soldiery, who "rightly suspected him of treachery to the Khalsa."[4] His body was burnt on the plain outside the Lahore fort on September 22, 1845. Two wives and three slave-girls became *satīs*. They begged for their lives, but were forced in procession between the army's ranks

[1] Viscount Hardinge, *Lord Hardinge* ("Rulers of India"), 165

[2] *The Jummoo and Kashmir Territories* (1875), 52.

[3] *Ranjit Singh*, 65.

[4] *Ibid.*

The trays from which they were to make the *satī's* customary distribution of jewels and money were snatched from their attendants, their own personal ornaments taken, and even their ear-rings torn out. We are told that the pillage continued even after the pyre had been lit, and that soldiers tried to rescue the gold fringing of the women's trousers, and that even in the flames one of the *satīs* rose and cursed her persecutors. The *satīs'* cries and appeals on the way to the pile were answered with jest and ribaldry. For a crime so terrible and open, the slaughter of the Khalsa in its war with the British a few months later seemed a just retribution.

"A *satī* is considered a sacred object among Hindus, and her last words prophetic. At the feet of these wretched women, Raja Dina Nath, who was officially present on behalf of the Rani, and many others fell down, imploring their blessings. The *satīs* blessed him and the Maharaja, but cursed the army of the Khalsa. When asked the fate of the Punjab, they answered that during the year the country would lose its independence, the Khalsa be overthrown, and the wives of the men of the army would be widows. They were then forced into the flames of the funeral pile; but the prophecy came true, and no curse was more amply fulfilled." [1]

This scene had behind it a woman's cruelty. The wazir, whose execution had been irregular and sudden, was brother of Rani Jindan—equally entitled with him to the adjective "infamous." His death filled her with the wildest passion of grief, and she was

[1] For this and the next two quotations see Griffin, *Ranjit Singh*, 65–67.

resolved that his funeral should be one with all honours; but the army let their loathing of the dead man vent itself on the miserable chattels that his sister drove into the flames with him. It is pleasant to close the story of the Sikh suttees by an example which shows how loyalty and deep affection, when the object was worthy, could transfigure even this awful sacrifice. Sir Lepel Griffin, contrasting the last two suttees, says:

"The last two widow-burnings in the Punjab were remarkable as showing this curious Hindu custom at its worst and at its best; in other words, where the victims were brutally murdered in the name of religion, or where they voluntarily and cheerfully met the death of fire as the glorious crown of a life of self-sacrifice and devotion."

I will tell the story of the last [1] Panjab suttee in his words; it is that of the widow of Sardar Sham Singh, one of the noblest and best of the Sikhs, who was killed at Sobraon (February 10, 1846):

"He had denounced the war with the English, and well foresaw what its termination must be. But he resolved to fight for the Khalsa, and on the night before Sobraon he swore on the *Granth* never to leave the field defeated. In the morning he dressed himself in white, and, having mounted his white mare, addressed his men, begging them, as true sons of the Khalsa, to die rather than yield. During the first part of the battle he was everywhere present, urging

[1] So Griffin called it in 1898, and the *Oxford History of India* follows him. But it cannot have been, since it is understood that the Lawrences had great difficulty in suppressing suttee after the British occupation, though no writer gives any evidence of this. But see a letter by Henry Lawrence, written November 15, 1846 (*Life*, ii. 80), which shows it still survived.

the Sikhs to fight bravely; and it was not till he saw that all was lost that he spurred forward against the 50th Regiment, waving his sword and calling on his men to follow him. Some fifty of them obeyed the call, but were driven into the river Sutlej, and Sham Singh fell dead from his horse, pierced with seven bullets. After the battle his servants begged permission to search for his body. The old Sirdar, conspicuous by his white dress and long white beard, was discovered where the dead lay thickest. His servants placed the body on a raft and swam with it across the river; but it was not till the third day that it reached his home at Attari. His widow, who knew his resolution not to survive defeat, had already burnt herself with the clothes which the Sirdar had worn on his wedding-day. This was the last *satī* in the Punjab, and the pillar which marks the spot where it took place is still standing outside the walls of Attari."

During these last years of suttee in the Panjab it was equally prevalent in the states that lay between the Sikh kingdom and the British Raj. Some of these were tiny ones hidden in the Himalayas and at the doors of Simla; but three, the "Phulkian" states,[1] were Sikh states. The Phulkian states had accepted alliance with the British; but, with a storm obviously beating up from beyond the Sutlej, it was not advisable to press reforms upon them. Nevertheless, in 1833 the Patiala Agent drew the Maharaja's attention to suttees that had occurred in that state on May 20th and 31st; they had occurred close to Subathu, which had been a British cantonment since the Nepal war, though still part of Patiala. British prestige suffered when a rite forbidden by British

[1] Nabha, Patiala, Jhind.

law took place so near British settlements. The Maharaja, to placate the Agent, fined those responsible, though their action had been quite legal.

Suttee in Mandi, a Panjab hill state whose capital is less than fifty miles in a direct line from Simla, forced itself on British attention in these years. Sir William Lee-Warner and Viscount Hardinge both cite the burning of twelve women with a Mandi Raja as an outstanding case that troubled people who heard of it. Sir William gives no date, but his context implies that it happened between 1829 and 1835[1]; whilst Lord Hardinge definitely states[2] that it was in the Governor-Generalship of his relative, the first Lord Hardinge, 1844–1848. But only one Raja of Mandi died between 1829 and 1851; his death was in 1839, and we find our firm ground of evidence with G. T. Vigne, who in that year witnessed[3] a suttee in Mandi, a short time after the last ruler's funeral. He appealed in vain to the Raja to prevent the sacrifice. The Raja next day called upon him and explained that he could not interfere in such affairs; he was very affable, and they went on to discuss suttee as an adjunct of royal funerals:

"The Rajah also told me that the omission of the ceremony would be looked upon as an act of disrespect to the memory of a deceased Rajah; and of the truth of his assertion there could be no doubt. I had seen the tombs of the Rajahs

[1] *The Native States of India*, 304.

[2] *Lord Hardinge* ("Rulers of India"), 165.

[3] I have quoted part of his account in the Appendix.

of Mundi by the roadside, a few hundred yards from the entrance to the town. The place of their ashes is marked by a long, narrow stone slab, standing upright in the ground, and on each of them is sculptured, in relief, a small sitting figure of the deceased, attended by other figures in the same attitude, purporting to represent the *satīs* who were burnt with him. The number of female figures varied, but none of the later Rajahs had fewer than twenty disposed in rows above and below him. The late Rajah had been dead but three months, and the puppet representations of no less than twenty-five women who had been burnt with him were evidently freshly produced by the rude chisel of the Mundi sculptor."[1]

After Sobraon the Sikh Government surrendered, and Sir Henry Lawrence was appointed Resident and President of a Council of Regency, the Maharaja being under age. Lawrence was the real ruler, and attempted "to conduct the administration on more or less civilized lines."[2] Suttee, accordingly, disappeared from the Panjab, though not at once.

It disappeared also from all but one of the minor Sikh states, and from the nest of petty hill states. Already, on April 12, 1843, the Thakur of Tiroj, accepting the British Government as entitled to settle a succession quarrel, had received a *sanad* from it and promised to suppress suttee. At the close of the first Sikh war the same engagement was required both from those states on the upper Sutlej that had been under British protection before and from those that had only now exchanged the over-

[1] *Travels in Kashmir, Ladak, Iskardo* (1842), 85.
[2] *Oxford History of India*, 695.

MEMORIAL STONES OF THE MANDI RAJAS

lordship of Lahore for that of Calcutta. On October 24, 1846, the Rajas of Suket and of Mandi promised to abolish suttee. The engagements entered into by these fierce little kingdoms usually discriminated against more than suttee—with reason. Thus the Raja of Mandi promised:

> "He shall so put a stop to the practices of slave-dealing, suttee, female infanticide, and the burning or drowning of lepers, which are opposed to British laws, that no one shall venture in future to revive them." [1]

Often mutilation was added to the list of practices proscribed.

Between September 1847 and April 1848, Patiala, Bilaspur, Faridkot, Jhind, and Chamba all promised to forbid suttee and its kindred abominations. One Sikh state, Nabha, apparently did not promise until May 5, 1860.

## Suttee in Rajasthan.

Meanwhile in Rajasthan suttee continued almost unchecked, Udaipur retaining its sombre pre-eminence. A writer in the *Asiatic Journal*, 1835, describing the city, speaks of the rite as in its immemorial abundant practice. "Those whose minds are made up" loosed their tresses and emptied a pot of water over them; after this there was no retreat from the pyre. The state, as for many years previously, and as it was to continue for another thirty years, until the British

[1] *Treaties, Engagements, and Sunnuds*, vi. 144.

Government imperiously called both parties to order, was the scene of incessant squabbles between the Maharana and his nobles; the country remained impoverished, with its internal resources wasting and its tribute heavily in arrears and its administration backward and bigoted. One extravagant and debauched ruler succeeded to another. On March 31, 1828, Maharana Bhim Singh died,

> "having learnt neither humility from affliction nor wisdom from poverty. He held fast by his faults and weaknesses to his death, and he was accompanied to the funeral pyre by four wives and four concubines." [1]

His successor, Jawan Singh, gave himself up to ten years of vice and debauchery. His funeral rites call for something more than passing mention.

> "On the 30th of August, 1838, the princely city of Oodypore was the scene of a terrible solemnity. About midday a prolonged discharge of artillery from the fort announced the unexpected decease of Maharana Juwan Singh; and, as is usual in tropical climates, preparations for his obsequies immediately commenced. The palace gate was thronged with the exultant populace. Something, however, in the excitement of their voices and gestures boded the approach of a spectacle more thrilling than mere pomp could render even a royal funeral. It was not the dead alone whom the eager crowd were waiting to see pass from among them. Sculptured in startling abundance on the tombs of their rulers, the well-known effigies of *women's feet* gave ghastly assurance that a prince of Oodypore would not that day be gathered to his fathers without a wife, or a concubine, sharing his pyre. The only question was—how many? It

[1] *The Rajputana Gazetteer, Mewar Agency.* The Resident at Delhi, writing to Fort William (Calcutta) on April 9, 1828, says seven ranis and one favourite concubine.

was known that the youngest of the two queens came of a family in which the rite was rarely practised; while the suddenness of the Maharana's death had given but scanty time for any of his inferior women to mature so tremendous a resolution. Great, therefore, was the admiration of the multitude when they learnt that, immediately on the fatal tidings reaching the zenana, both the queens and six out of seven concubines had determined to burn. . . .

"The eight victims, dressed in their richest attire and mounted on horseback, moved with the procession to the cemetery. There they stripped off their ornaments and jewels, distributed gifts to the bystanders, and lastly, mounting the pile, took their places beside the corpse. As the Maharana had left no son, his nephew, the present sovereign, applied the torch. The crash of music, the chanting of the priests, and the cries of the multitude arose simultaneously, and the tragedy was consummated. 'The father of one of the queens' (concludes the native report) 'was present during the whole. He is here immersed in contemplation and grief, and his companions are comforting him.'"[1]

Lord Auckland, through the Resident at Udaipur, unofficially expressed displeasure at the barbarity and at the prominent part taken by the new Rana. Udaipur shrugged its shoulders and went its blood-strewn way. Four years later the new Maharana, Sardar Singh, died. Again it was unthinkable that a Chief of Mewar should go to the pyre without "the dreadful honours of the *satī* sacrifice."[2] But his

[1] H. J. Bushby, *Widow-Burning*, 5–6. The author makes certain mistakes. For example, when his book was published (1855) the Maharana was the successor of the one who applied the torch. Also, nine women became *satis*, and not eight. And "women's feet" mark the suttee memorials of the Maratha country, rarely those of Rajasthan.

[2] Cunningham's phrase in connection with the funeral of Jawahir Singh (*History of the Sikhs*, edited by H. L. O. Garrett, Clarendon Press, 272).

reign had been one of incessant quarrelling with his nobles, who strongly disliked him, and

> "his personal unpopularity was emphasized, even when he was no longer among the living, by none save one lady consenting to be burned with his corpse." [1]

The *Guidebook's* euphemism veils the plain fact that public opinion would not have tolerated that a Rana's funeral should be one of his dead body alone, without a female chattel to keep it company. The growing unwillingness to burn manifested at this time by Indian ladies, even by Sikh and Rajput ladies, shows that they were influenced by the knowledge that outside their narrow barbarous world was an India from which suttee had passed away.

On September 5, 1843, Man Singh, Maharaja of Jodhpur, died. One lady with the rank of queen, four concubines and a slave-girl burned with him. The reader of Tod will remember this Man Singh and the part he had played in the miseries of Rajasthan thirty-seven years previously. He had lingered on into this new age, when the old India was breaking up, and his death-pomp was with the rites of that older world. That older world had yet another fourteen years of shorn and uncertain existence to run before the Mutiny swept it away and modern India came into being.

The Rajputs have had "a good press" in the West, but it is nothing to the press they have had

[1] *Udaipur Guidebook.*

in India. The heroic and terrible history and legends of Mewar furnish the stuff for the most popular plays of vernacular theatres, especially among the peaceable but (in their literature) gore-loving Bengalis. These plays, and the kindred novels, treat their themes in a mood of imbecile exultation and adoration. So far as I have had means to judge, no breath of criticism or sanity has yet blown in upon Indian thought where Rajasthan is concerned. The story, as Indian writers tell it, is without human interest, the dramas are without probability, character-differentiation, poetry, or common sense. Once the story of Rajasthan is faced by minds really moving in this modern world, that story will produce plays and fiction which will cause the extant trash to be tossed on the rubbish-heap where it belongs. Indian writers pay no true homage to the valour of Rajasthan, and no just tribute to the pity of its fate, when they represent its people as demigods with the minds of savage children.

It was this idealization of Udaipur that made the efforts of the British Government to extirpate suttee in native states so slow in meeting with success. For,

"whatever a Hindoo knows of chivalry or nationality, he deems to be exemplified in this model race. Since, therefore, Rajpoots were renowned for the frequency of their suttees, the great independent states thought it beneath their orthodoxy to return any other answer to the remonstrances of the British Government against the rite than that 'it would be time enough for them to prohibit it when Rajpootana led the way.'"[1]

[1] Bushby, 11.

But, as in the years preceding Bentinck's abolition of the sacrifice, so now, individual officers were sometimes able to do more than Government felt entitled to attempt. The Resident at Kotah obtained an evasive promise from the Raja that he would do his best to stop the rite. A few months later, on October 29, 1840, the Raja refused to act, and a Brahman's widow burned. The first substantial Rajput success came at Jaipur. Major Ludlow, in the Maharaja's minority, was President of the Council of Regency. He first persuaded the Rajput states to abolish female infanticide; then, in 1846, after long endeavour, his tact and personal popularity won the Jaipur Council over as to suttee also. Already some of the powerful Jaipur nobles had suppressed it in their own territories; but his success with the Council took everybody by surprise, his predecessor as Resident most of all. Lord Hardinge, the Governor-General, notified the prohibition in the *Gazette*, September 22, 1846, thanking Ludlow for his service. The example set by Jaipur, a state second only to Udaipur in influence, was quickly followed. Before Christmas 1846 eleven of the eighteen Rajput states and five independent states outside Rajasthan forbade suttee. Kotah suppressed it next year (March 1847), and Jodhpur in the time of Hardinge's successor, Dalhousie. The reader, noting these dates, will note also that the end of the first Sikh war opened on a period of very vigorous administrative activity, when every effort was made to stamp out surviving inhumanities. The fact that the British had defeated the great Sikh confederacy strengthened their prestige enormously, and made even Rajput states willing to meet their prejudices. In fact, it is not too much to say that it was the victory over the Khalsa that alone made any sort of move against suttee in Rajasthan possible at all. From first to last Rajasthan had been the metropolis of the rite, as it had almost certainly been the original home from which it had spread over India millenniums before. The Sikh practice of suttee had been an aberration, contrary to the teaching of some of their Gurus. Outside Rajasthan, the ruling families of Rewa Kanta, as well as those of Idar and Ahmadnagar, were nearly all Rajput;[1] and it was only the accident of these states being near enough to cause annoyance to the Bombay Government by encouraging British subjects in the forbidden practice that had led to interference in Rewa Kanta.

If the honour of the abolition within British India is Bentinck's, that of the final suppression of suttee by native states is largely Dalhousie's. Though practically no promises were made in his time, he insisted that promises already made must be kept, and those who broke them punished. To the extreme limits of his power he acted with ruthless vigour. The ruthlessness was necessary, for in the Rajput tradition, along with magnificent qualities, was a

[1] The ruling race in Nepal is Rajput by origin.

barbarism so deep-rooted that only a sterner fierceness could extirpate it. The *Encyclopædia Britannica* says that in native states "suttee he kept down with an iron hand."[1] Like almost every statement on the subject, this needs qualification, which Dalhousie's own Minute of February 28, 1856 (paragraph 146), reviewing his administration, supplies:

> "The prohibition of suttee by the British Government is now a familiar tale. In the time of those who preceded me great progress had been made in persuading all native princes to unite in denouncing the rite and in punishing those who should disregard the prohibition. The Government of India, since 1848, has had only to follow up the measures of preceding years. When suttee has occurred in an independent state, no opportunity of remonstrating has been lost. When it has occurred in any district which was within our control, no indulgence has been shown to the culprits. Thus renewed remonstrances have been addressed to Ulwar, Beeckaneer and Oodeypore; but in Doongurpore, a British state under our direct management, where a thakoor's son took part in a suttee, the son and a Brahmin who abetted his crime were condemned to imprisonment for three years in irons; while the thakoor himself, for the same three years, was mulcted in half the revenue of his possession. The performance of suttee is now a rare occurrence, either in Mahomedan or native states."

Dungarpur, a tiny Rajput state, was temporarily dependent on the Imperial authority, its chief being a minor. But I cannot find the proof, with regard to the three powerful recalcitrant states, Udaipur, Alwar, and Bikanir, either of the *Encyclopædia Britannica's* statement or of Trotter's:

[1] Article "Dalhousie."

"In Udaipur, Alwar, and Bikanir, Lord Dalhousie's interference took the form of threats, which the native princes and chiefs had the wisdom to accept as positive commands." [1]

In the case of Alwar and Bikanir, the support of suttee was one of theory rather than of practice.[2] Before Dalhousie came, Alwar had abandoned the rite at the funeral of its rulers; and in Bikanir the last "distinguished *satī*" [3] was Dip Kunwar, a daughter of the Udaipur ruling family and wife of Maharaja Surat Singh's second son, Moti Singh. She died in 1825, and a fair is still held in her honour at Devi Kund, a village five miles east of Bikanir. But so long as suttee was legal it was bound to occur; it continued to occur even in parts of Rajasthan where it was forbidden, as when the sister-in-law of the Bhinai Raja burned in Ajmer in 1857. She exercised a *satī's* immemorial right of curse and blessing, for the Brahmans who attended her to the pyre begged her to pronounce against the unpopular cess with which the British Agent supported the schools. In 1857 the British Government was in no case to take the field against suttee in loyal states, even when it was forbidden by law. The *satī* won a victory for her people; the cess was withdrawn.

Whatever assurance Dalhousie may have thought he had obtained from Udaipur, after he had gone

[1] *India under Victoria*, i. 258.

[2] This was true of every Indian state except Udaipur (and, of course, Nepal) in 1855.

[3] *Imperial Gazetteer of India* (1908).

the state swung back, and in 1861 Maharana Sarup Singh's funeral was disgraced by the murder of a slave-girl. More than thirty years had passed since suttee had been made illegal in British India, and eighteen since slavery had been abolished. This sacrifice *may* be the one Mr. Kipling had in mind in his poem, *The Last Suttee,* but there is no resemblance between the two stories except the fact that a slave-girl died. In every other detail they contradict each other utterly, and the geography of his poem, though picturesque, is absurd, making the Boondi King lord of many lands to which he had no manner of claim and which were far from his own. I mention this, not as criticizing Mr. Kipling, but because readers seem to think that his poem gives a historical account of a real suttee, and that one the last. As the last suttee at the funeral of a reigning chief of protected India, the Udaipur one deserves that we should read of it in a nearly contemporary official document.

"After the demise of the last Maharana of Udaipur, the first Hindu prince of India, the acknowledged head of the Rajputs, and the ruler of a principality wherein ancient customs and usages are cherished more religiously than perhaps in any other State, each wife was successively asked to preserve the honour of the Sesodia tribe, the chief of which had never burnt alone. One and all most positively declined, and a favourite slave-girl was then appealed to by her brother! In speaking to the wretched girl, he dwelt strongly upon the fact that all the late chief's lawfully married queens had refused to preserve the honour of the house, and that the greater credit would redound upon her were she prepared to set an example of devotion to those who so wilfully declined to evince any themselves; that their perversity, in short, had afforded her an opportunity to earn a world-wide reputation for fidelity, which it were madness to neglect. His arguments prevailed. . . . The royal corpse, dressed up in regal attire, was conveyed from the palace to the burning-place (called the Mahasati) in a species of sedan-chair; the funeral procession, composed of all loyal subjects of the state, one and all, high and low, even the successor to the throne, proceeded the whole distance on foot; one alone in this vast multitude was allowed to ride, and she had but a short time to live. Mounted on a gorgeously caparisoned horse, herself richly attired as for a festive occasion, literally covered with jewels and costly ornaments, her hair loose and in disorder, her whole countenance wild with the excitement of the scene and the intoxicating effects of the drugs she had swallowed, she issued forth with the body. As customary on such occasions, the victim, as the procession moved on, unclasped the ornaments with which she was profusely decorated and flung them to the right and to the left amongst the crowd. On reaching the Mahasati, in a space enclosed by tent walls, the corpse was unrobed, and the slave-girl, seating herself with the head of the lifeless body in her lap, was built up, as it were, with wood steeped in oil. The *kanats*, or canvas walls, were then removed and the pyre lighted; and as the flame shot up bright and fierce the crowd around raised a great clamour, which lasted until the dreadful scene was over. . . .

"Shocking as this *satī* was felt to be, the fact that every wife had, for the first time in the annals of Mewar, declined to die on such an occasion cannot but react favourably on the feelings and sentiments of other Rajput families." [1]

The Mutiny was one of those rare episodes that are not only impressive in themselves, but mark the end

[1] *Report on the Political Administration of Rajputana*, 1865–1867, by Colonel W. F. Eden, Agent of the Governor-General.

of an era. It left the native chieftains dependent on the paramount Power as they had never been before—no longer princes, but at best barons. Those that kept their status were those that had shown themselves friendly to the British Raj; their salutes were augmented, but no additional ceremonial could keep their real importance undiminished. Inevitably, popular sympathy had been with the insurgents, and those chieftains who had helped the British were aware that they were out of favour with their country, even with their own subjects. They had to draw closer to the protecting Power, and in subtle ways this sense of dependence moulded even their deepest and oldest prejudices. They could not ignore the strong feeling of the British Government even in such an immemorial custom as suttee. The Udaipur suttee of 1861 was an isolated instance—the last. It was possible, partly because during the Mutiny Udaipur, by giving asylum to British families, had established a claim on the gratitude of the Supreme Government, partly because the state was in a condition almost of anarchy, in which old traditions alone were powerful and no one could be made responsible. Between 1860 and 1862 the British Government overhauled its relations with the native states; *sanads* were given, guaranteeing and defining the status of each, and engagements were taken. The lesser states renewed their promises to prohibit suttee; and, though such a promise was not required explicitly from the greater states, we may take it that it was understood between the contracting parties that suttee was to cease. Sarup Singh was succeeded in Udaipur by a minor, and the real power rested with the Political Agent; even so, the Council was found inefficient and unsatisfactory, so that it was "found necessary to entrust greater power to the Agent,"[1] who proceeded to introduce many reforms and to pull the state out of its long-continued anarchy. The revenues were managed so economically, that when the Rana took over the government, in November 1865, there was a balance in the treasury; life and property were made secure, and the law courts overhauled. The fourteen first-class nobles now try all cases of crime or complaint in which both parties are their subjects; but cases of murder, *satī*, highway robbery with violence, traffic in children, and coining have to be reported, and the barons' decisions submitted for the Maharana's approval.

We are justified, then, in taking 1862 as the approximate date when suttee became illegal in Rajasthan and in states where it had already fallen into desuetude—Kashmir, Bhopal, and Bharatpur. It became "illegal" in this sense, that the paramount Power would not have tolerated its continued existence; and it ceased because Rajput ladies refused to mount the pyre.

The story of the suppression of suttee in native

[1] *Rajputana Gazetteer, Mewar Residency.*

states is one of the minor stories of Indian history, and one that has never been told, partly because the Imperial Government keeps its correspondence with the greater states strictly secret, and the tale of what happened is scattered over many hundreds of memoirs, district gazetteers, and contemporary newspapers, most of which have long ago perished and survive only in some quoted scrap. The story has not the obvious importance that attaches to that of a great campaign in the field, but I think that there is no story that more clearly brings out the watchfulness and courage that were required in the thirty years during which British officers, bound by their instructions—which were rarely exceeded, and then only for such terrible reason as Erskine had at Ahmadnagar—not to go beyond verbal and diplomatic protest, slowly and patiently persuaded princes to abandon their most cherished honour. If the British Government were needlessly timid in prohibiting suttee in British India, and delayed this act of humanity by many unnecessary years, they made amends by the persistence with which they took their opportunities in the native states in the thirty years following their own prohibition.

## CHAPTER IX

# ILLEGAL SUTTEE

### IN NATIVE STATES.

THOUGH 1861 was the date of the last suttee at the funeral of a ruling prince, the rite died hard, and often swelled the death-pomp of a Rajput *thākur* or baron. The late Colonel Eckford Luard gave me the note:

> "Before our greater interference in state affairs had come —say, from 1880 on—*thākurs*, especially big landholders, were practically independent within their estates. Now this is no longer so, as state administrations are assimilating themselves to ours—far too much so, I think! They are losing that elasticity, wrongly called 'want of efficiency,' which is really the human touch in administration—even if in some directions it is occasionally rather perverted humanity!"

I give some examples of the Rajput suttees that sprinkle the last forty years of the century. I have referred to the remarkable one in Ajmer in 1857. In 1862 there was a *satī* at the funeral of the *thākur* of Rewa in Sirohi; the persons responsible were punished by imprisonment. In June 1864 the widow of the son of the *thākur* of Begun, in Udaipur, was burnt, as was the widow of Sham Singh, the *thākur* of Utarna, in Jaipur, in 1883. The latter instance resulted in sentences of seven years' rigorous imprisonment for the sons and brothers of the husband and three years for minor accomplices. The last suttee in Central India took place in the Rajput state of Datia [1] in 1895.

There have been suttees in other states also. I mention two late occurrences of the rite. On October 1, 1853, the widow of the Waghela chief of Aluwa, in Kuri, a district in the Gaekwar's dominions, burned; and in 1860 there was a suttee of extreme atrocity near Guna, in Gwalior. The widow's resolution failed her, and she escaped from the burning pile; the spectators struck her with sticks and twice wounded her with swords, but she was maddened and managed to hide in reeds on the banks of the river Parvati. She was discovered, dragged out, and drowned.

## In British India.

The learned Judge who tried the appeal of Ram Dayal before the Allahabad High Court in 1913 noted that

> "the Regulation of 1829 seems to have had immediate effect, and the practice was almost completely stamped out. In fact, I can only find three reported cases of *satī* in the Law Reports for these provinces and for Bengal since that date. They occurred in 1834, 1854, and 1871."

I do not understand this summary; illegal suttee was much commoner than this, especially if we

[1] For this information I am indebted to Colonel Luard.

include cases followed by no prosecution. In the first few years after prohibition it might almost be called common.

Mr. Coomaraswamy, in a footnote to the passage that I have quoted at the beginning of this study, reminds us:

> "'Social conventions' are rarely '*man*-made laws' alone." [1]

That is true; and when suttee was first prohibited, widows, disconsolate at deprivation of the right to burn with their husbands, sometimes starved themselves to death. The *Chandrikā* composed some suitable elegiacs on one such case that occurred in Bengal in 1830:

> "Words cannot express the distress we have felt on hearing this intelligence; for in this case a virtuous and faithful wife has given up life, after great mental compunction, through the irresistible prohibitions imposed in regard of suttees by Government. Yet this virtuous woman after her death has attained felicity, for the husband is the only instructor, the only God of a wife; for that blessed woman, overwhelmed with various anxieties, though she was not able to burn her own body with that of her husband, reflecting on her husband's feet as though they were her tutelary deity, has liberated herself from the body by refusing food. Yet it is a matter of the deepest regret to us. How the children to whom she gave birth are able now to drag on their existence it is beyond our power to say. . . . What shall we say to them? It was beyond their power to burn their mother. It is customary for those in deep distress to make it known to the sovereign; but the sovereign of this country is himself become the destroyer of this practice."

---

[1] *The Dance of Siva*, 91.

But our old friend the *Kaumudī*, on October 15th of the same year, brought forward another case, in which the widow had stopped short of tragedy:

> 'After two days her hunger overcame her sorrow, and she with much importunity and distress requested some food, which was brought to her immediately. From that day she has remained contentedly with her family and busied herself with the work of the house."

To show how stubbornly suttee persisted I give a few examples from the early days of prohibition. In January 1830, in the Tirhut zila of Patna, a widow appealed to the *dārogā* (head constable) who tried to stop her from the pile and won him over. She burned herself, and the *dārogā* lost his post. There were suttees at Ratnagiri (February 1830); Chibotu, in Patna (May 10, 1830); Madhurikand, thirty-five miles north-east of Agra (September 16, 1831); near Gaya in 1832; at Muttra (May 13, 1833). The reader should note the frequency with which places in Bihar recur in connection with suttee; the district has had several suttees in the present century. The Madhurikand case resulted in a prosecution; three men were sentenced to seven years' imprisonment, two to five years'. But the High Court reduced the sentences, and the Governor-General pardoned all except one of the accused, who was captured after absconding and received a year's hard labour. Next year, 1832, the first case from Bengal to be tried under the new Regulation reached the courts; the accused pleaded, and the plea was allowed, that the village authorities had not promulgated the Regulation. But the excuse that they did not know that suttee was illegal was pushed aside by a higher court. Ultimately Lord Bentinck pardoned them personally.

In these early years of prohibition the name of Angria's Kolaba frequently occurs. This is an island twenty miles from Bombay, formerly the haunt of a pirate chief Angria. For many years, as I have mentioned in Chapter VIII, widows from Bombay and other British territory were taken here and burnt. I find such instances in contemporary newspapers mentioned as having occurred in August 1830 and in 1834. The *Bombay Gazette*, commenting on the latter case, says that the practice was common. The chieftains ruling other adjacent territories gave the same hospitality to suttee, as we have seen.

In addition to the few cases that reached the law courts, or were authenticated by clear report, there can be no doubt that suttee often occurred undetected and unpunished. A missionary writes (June 27, 1845):

> "A short time since a suti was performed in a village near, almost under the eyes of the authorities, yet the murderers could not be found out." [1]

Careful search shows suttee, though quickly growing rare, still from time to time recurring. I have found

[1] *Memoir of J. J. Weitbrecht*, 159. He is writing of the Burdwan district of Bengal.

one case in the Mutiny area during the Mutiny period —a bad case in the Farakhabad district in 1858. Suttee has persisted into the present century. Bihar had cases in 1901, 1903, 1904, 1905; there was one in a small village in the Panjab in 1905; and in 1906 there were suttees at Cawnpore and in Calcutta. Sixteen persons were charged in connection with the 1903 Bihar case, which occurred in the village of Kaltaki, Gaya district. In the 1904 case, which was a suttee in the Patna district,

> "Among the articles in evidence" (i.e. at the trial) "there was an invitation issued by the son to the sraddha in which it was stated that his father was dead and his mother had become a satti. Another document showed the line of defence to be taken in case of prosecution." [1]

That line of defence was the usual one—one that came up frequently even before Bentinck's Regulation of 1829, whenever some illegality of detail brought the supervisors of a suttee into court: the widow had persisted in burning herself and had perished by spontaneous combustion, which was supposed to occur with exceptionally holy *satīs*. But it was made clear that the spectators provided a great deal of assistance by pouring *ghi* and other inflammable substances on the widow and by throwing wood on the bodies. What cannot be considered too deeply is that no one considered he had done anything wrong by helping in the act, and that these suttees

[1] Sir Andrew Fraser, *Among Indian Rajahs and Ryots*, 102.

gave intense delight to Hindus who read of them and almost delirious pleasure to the spectators. Within a very few hours of the death of the Patna district *satī* a shrine had been made and lamps were burning in her honour ; booths and shops were erected to supply the needs of pilgrims.

The classical instance of illegal suttee took place in the Allahabad district in 1913. I propose to treat this interesting case at some length, quoting and condensing from the judgment of the Court of Appeal.

Ram Lal, a Brahman resident in the village of Jarauli, died early in the morning of June 27, 1913. He had been ill for some months, and his widow's intention to become a *satī* was well known. Her relations and neighbours failed to dissuade her, and sent the *chaukidār* to the police-station, eight miles away, to give warning. They meanwhile hurried on preparations for the funeral, and with quite unnecessary haste completed the double burning before noon. The accused persons prepared the pyre, which the widow walked round seven times in orthodox fashion and then mounted. She then stripped off her ornaments, which she threw into a cloth held by the two principal accused. She demanded *ghi*, which was given, and which she poured over herself and the pyre.

Five persons were convicted, and the Sessions Judge sentenced Ram Dayal and Dodraj to two years' rigorous imprisonment and three minor offenders to one and a half years. They appealed, and the Judge of the High Court issued notice to them to show cause why the sentences should not be enhanced. After re-trial, the lesser sentences were confirmed, and that on Ram Dayal and Dodraj enhanced to four years' rigorous imprisonment.

The defence alleged gross negligence on the part of the police in arriving late, and that they themselves had acted under fear, the *satī* having threatened to curse them if they withheld assistance. The morning that she died she had shown her chastity by many miraculous deeds—she had held burning camphor in her two hands clapped together, she had smitten an impudent girl into a fit with a glance of her eyes and had restored her again, and she had made the rain cease at about nine o'clock. The sympathies of the witnesses were with the accused, and they refused to say who had fired the pile. The two principal accused

> admitted carrying out certain details under her orders; but knew that these would be infructuous without the final act of setting fire, which they never did. . . . Both the witnesses and the accused stated that when all was ready and the widow demanded fire, Ram Dayal and Dodraj refused to give it to her, telling her that if there were any virtue in her she could produce it for herself, whereupon she whispered into the ear of the corpse, and, raising her arms aloft, prayed to God, and shortly after the pyre burst into flame.

The learned Judge pointed out that the whole country-side had been roused, and that there were fifteen hundred to two thousand spectators, many of whom must have come from a distance. Further:

> A very little force would have been necessary to prevent the woman ascending the pyre. Moreover, it was not absolutely necessary to burn the corpse at so early an hour. Though information had been sent to the police, no serious attempt was made to await their arrival on the scene. Sixteen miles had to be walked before they could arrive, and the accused must have known that no police officer could possibly arrive until after midday. . . .
>
> Any relaxation of the severity of the law in such a matter will result in the recurrence of the evil which took so many years to decrease to a minimum. The feelings and beliefs which prompt a *satī* still exist, and but little encouragement was needed to revive the rite. In conclusion:
>
> *Satī* may or may not be forbidden by the Hindu religion, but it was once a common practice, and the sympathies of the people, at least of the unenlightened people, are all with *satī* and it is looked upon as a meritorious deed.

There have also been many instances of private suttee. Some of these have shown extraordinary determination, as one that occurred in the Tinneveli district of South India in 1876.[1] The widow dug a pit inside her house, filled it with sandalwood, and dressed herself as a bride; she shut the doors, lit the pile, and leapt in. This case is the stranger in that Tinneveli is not a district where suttee lingered with any great persistence, though it is close to Madura and Tanjore, where suttee had been an apanage of kings and nobles.

[1] *Globe*, January 10, 1877.

The commonest form of irregular suttee is when a woman drenches her clothes with paraffin and burns herself in her own home. Such suttees have been fairly frequent. One occurred in Calcutta in 1911; there was a rush of hysterical women to the place to pick up relics, especially fragments of the vermilion lac. I well remember the imbecile enthusiasm of the Bengali press.

No doubt there are suttees of this kind that never come to official notice, and these may sometimes be compulsory. Mrs. Sinclair-Stevenson,[1] asking what became of unwanted widows, often had the reply, "Paraffin is cheap." But I do not think such immolations are anything like as common as she fears, or as the latest writer on suttee, Mr. N. M. Penzer,[2] seems to think on her authority. And these are crimes on the borderland between suttee and ordinary brutal murder, and as such hardly call for more than slanting notice in this study.

It is impossible to collect or collate all the evidence of illegal suttee in British India and native states; but I think it would be easy to show that suttee, in one form or another, public or private and irregular, has occurred almost every year in some part of India between 1829 and 1913; and probably it will still occur, though at longer intervals.

[1] See *Rites of the Twice-Born*, 207–8.
[2] See "Suttee" essay in *The Ocean of Story*, vol. iv.

## CHAPTER X

# LEGAL SUTTEE TO-DAY

IN Nepal, which is outside British jurisdiction, suttee is still legal. Mr. W. Crooke, in 1906, writes that "the rite still survives."[1] But very little information about the country gets outside Nepal.

Sir Jung Bahadur, the famous soldier and statesman who helped the British in the Mutiny, discountenanced suttee, so that the practice became rare; but his own funeral, in 1877, was a magnificent affair, with three *satīs*. This is often said to have been the last instance of suttee in Nepal; I am sure that it was not, but have no definite information.

After its virtual extinction in India, suttee flourished still in the hinduized islands of Bali and Lombok, as it had formerly flourished in Java. Slaves were burnt, wives were burnt or, especially in Bali, butchered with the "krîss," the Malay knife. Horrible accounts exist of widows slowly and clumsily slaughtered, the spectators indifferent or laughing. As in India, suttee was chiefly to glorify rajas, whose funerals were never without these sacrifices, to which priests' widows were not liable. The *Encyclopædia Britannica* speaks of suttee as still practised in these

[1] *Things Indian*, 449.

islands; so do other authorities, whom I quote with hesitation, as I doubt if they have more information than I have myself. "It is believed still to take place in noble families."[1] "The custom of widow-burning is still occasionally practised"[2] (in Bali).

[1] Sir Charles Eliot, *Hinduism and Buddhism* (1921), iii. 183.
[2] N. M. Penzer, in *The Ocean of Story* (1926), iv. 257.

## CHAPTER XI

# CONCLUDING CONSIDERATIONS

I HAVE not conducted this enquiry into an obscure subject from any love for the gruesome or the cruel, or only because in India the stories and traditions of suttee stirred profound pity in my mind and made me wish to win for its victims at least this posthumous justice, that their fate should not be misunderstood. I believe that the history of the rite sheds light on dark passages of Indian and British relations, and on certain periods and personalities of the last century; also that conclusions of value for to-day can be drawn.

### EFFECT OF SUTTEE ON EUROPEANS.

Suttee, as Sir Vernon Lovett remarked to me, by arousing the disgust and abhorrence of Englishmen who saw it or were contemporary with it, caused them to do injustice to Indian thought. It was impossible to think of Indian civilization as anything but a barbarian civilization. Macaulay's often-abused Minute about the relative value of Sanskrit literature and of "a single shelf" of modern European books had this background of barbarities shadowing his mind. If it was a mistake to set Indian education on solely Western lines, it was a mistake for which

Indians had themselves to thank, for the fruits of Hinduism a century ago were bad. As an Indian student of mine, a fervent Hindu, said to me, "A hundred years ago, not only Christian missionaries, but the early Brahmos also, thought that Hinduism was idolatrous." That is so; they also thought it cruel. There is a simple explanation of both beliefs, strange as they seem to neo-Hindus and theosophists to-day. Hinduism was what it seemed to be.

There were many other barbarities practised in India a century ago; but some might be dismissed as mere superstition, or as the crimes of backward tribes and perverted sects of Hinduism, such as those who practised human sacrifice. Infanticide had an economic cause. But suttee cut to the very roots of social morality, and the society which practised it and gloried in it made itself an outcast from the civilized comity of nations. It is often made a reproach against the British that, after a century and a half of predominance in India, they have not advanced the people any further along the road of fitness for self-government. I am not, I think, likely to ignore or forget the mistakes and shortcomings of our administration. But India's primary need to-day is fair judgment—from us to it and from it to us. And if we have written Indian history with unfairness, Indians have with equal unfairness put upon us the blame for many things for which they have been responsible. I have no doubt whatever that such things as suttee kept back Indian political progress by many years; until the rite was abolished, even a beginning in self-government was impossible.

> "To put the matter in a lower but a very practical light, we say that advancement of natives to high posts of emolument or responsibility was simply impossible while such relics of dark ages and dark superstitions were fostered or endured. The most grotesque and horrible incongruities would arise had suttee kept pace with our avowed and earnest desire to see natives taking a larger share in the government of the country. Imagine a native gentleman dying who was a member of the Governor-General's Council for making laws, and the Viceroy, on sending a message of condolence to his family, being quietly told that his wives had all burnt themselves the day before; or the native Justices of the Peace for the town of Calcutta stating their inability to attend a discussion on the waterworks of the metropolis because they wished to follow the widow of one of their number to her husband's pile at Chitpore or Garden Reach; or a Bengalee member of the Civil Service, for such there may be, refusing to subscribe to the civil fund because he would, under the Shastras, be only survived by his widow for the space of twelve hours! It was in one sense truly said that such practices were incompatible with the spread of education, but the sound rule, we submit, for our guidance would have been to put down violent crimes first and then educate and refine afterwards. The demoralization of the survivors entailed by the rite of suttee was palpably spreading, and was a worse feature than even the cruel tortures of the dying wife, which is saying a good deal." [1]

But India paid an immeasurable price, in other than practical ways, for the practice of suttee. The rite aroused in foreigners a contempt, especially in

[1] *Calcutta Review*, 1867, "Suttee."

Bengal, where the men were—and always had been—exempt from risk of death and maiming in battle, which is not yet eradicated. Its apologists and hymnists to-day are the large body of sentimentalists who are unteachably inaccurate, Europeans and Americans incapable of any intellectual process higher than unthinking ecstasy in the presence of what they imperfectly understand and wholly misrepresent, Indians incapable of any statement that is not tilted by some nationalist bias. India has been damned by the mental slackness of its exponents; we who love it are most of us people entitled to very little respect on intellectual grounds.

It may seem unjust and illogical that the Moguls, who freely impaled and flayed alive, or nationals of Europe, whose countries had such ferocious penal codes and had known, scarcely a century before suttee began to shock the English conscience, orgies of witch-burning and religious persecution, should have felt as they did about suttee. But the difference seemed to them this—the victims of their cruelties were tortured by a law which considered them offenders, whereas the victims of suttee were punished for no offence but the physical weakness which had placed them at man's mercy. The rite seemed to prove a depravity and arrogance such as no other human offence had brought to light.

"Something may be urged in support of every kind of custom, show, or amusement of a national character, however barbarous and demoralizing in many respects. In gladiatorial exhibitions, the old Romans, who, amidst all their fine qualities, had no sentiments of chivalry or generosity to the vanquished, learnt to admire the skill of the exhibitors, as well as the calm determination with which they passed by the Chief Magistrate, saluting him as dying men. In the bull-fights of Spain the adroitness of the matador sometimes half-drowns the pity felt for the mangled and disembowelled horses. Even at a prize-fight, gentlemen of taste and education have dwelt on the artistic position, the muscular, well-shaped, and healthy frame, and the exquisite skill in attack and defence manifested by the pugilists. Yet, in spite of skill and activity and heroic resolution, the almost universal consent of civilized nations now pronounces such spectacles to be barbarous and demoralizing. But in these cases the actors, anyhow, are men, strong and independent, and capable of judging for themselves. Suttees were made out of the weakest part of the creation. Illiterate women, preyed on by relatives, cowed by priests, morally if not physically drugged, were urged to continue to their husband after death that servile obedience to which they had been condemned in their lifetimes, or to encounter a state of dull and dreary widowhood to which death was almost preferable. Suttee appears to have sprung from, as well as to have perpetuated, some of the vilest feelings of our human nature. It began in selfishness, it was supported by falsehood, and it ended in cruelty such as might give support to fiends. No language is too strong for it. When we read the long record of human lives sacrificed to what was called our national good faith, the vacillating minutes, the elaborate reports, the indignant remonstrances which the subject excited, and the inactivity of a Government presided over at least by one able statesman, we can but sigh, as we read the blood-stained page, for one hour of either Bentinck or Dalhousie." [1]

Contemporary accounts of Bengal suttees a century ago, and the cases that, for one irregularity or another,

[1] *Calcutta Review*, 1867, "Suttee."

reached the courts, show that the rite was a huge public *tāmāshā*,[1] in which the lowest Mahommadans joined actively with the dregs of the Hindu populace.

### Bentinck and Dalhousie.

We have seen that we cannot claim the abolition of suttee as a triumph of "British justice" or an example of the righteous and fearless character of our administration. The garland belongs to one man almost alone, and no praise is too high for him.

Another thing that has become clear is the underlying motive of Dalhousie's annexations, some of them carried out against the strong disapproval of such men as Sir Henry Lawrence. His humanitarianism, reinforced and sharpened by his experience of the unwillingness of native states to set their houses in order in matters of elementary decency, was responsible for his anxiety to annex whenever possible. I believe that there was no "earth-hunger" behind his doctrine of "lapse"; and while criticizing him we should remember the exasperating refusal of many states to abolish suttee and female infanticide.

"A saying of his quoted by Hunter has, as that author observes, 'the ring of a great soul.'

"'I circulate these papers,' he wrote hastily on one case in which he had successfully insisted on justice being done at the risk of a tumult; 'they are an instance of the principle that we should do what is right without fear of consequences.

---

[1] Show.

To fear God and to have no other fear is a maxim of religion, but the truth of it and the wisdom of it are proved day by day in politics.' "[1]

## 1829 TO 1857.

We have further seen that the 1829 Regulation opened a period of intensive warfare against violent and cruel crime; British officers fought against dacoity, suttee, human sacrifice, thuggee, female infanticide. It was not kid-glove work; even the rites of the Aztecs were not more depraved and ferocious than those which marked the "meriah" human sacrifices of Orissa, and the officers who extirpated them were dealing with sub-human beings. Thuggee was stamped out by a ruthlessness that was unavoidable and well deserved.

"During the years 1831–1837, 3,266 thugs were disposed of in one way or another, 412 out of that number being hanged and 483 admitted as approvers. The approvers and their descendants were detained for many years in a special institution at Jubbulpore (Jabalpur)."[2]

The work of these years was largely summary; it necessarily developed the summary outlook and method. The period was marked also by four hard-fought wars—those with Sind, Gwalior, and the two Sikh wars—as well as two outside India, with Afghanistan and Burma. The summary mind was working in the aggression which forced Afghanistan

[1] *Oxford History of India*, 709. [2] *Ibid.*, 668.

and Sind to fight us, and in the annexations that made the period one of growing exasperation against the foreigner. The summary mind, when it is an individual dealing with unwilling and wild subjects, becomes the gamekeeper mind. These years, which saw province after province added to British India—Sind, the cis-Sutlej lands, and the Jullunder Doab, Kashmir, Hazara, the Panjab itself, Oudh—saw the improvisation of a loose and mainly personal system of administration for the vast tracts and fierce frontier where Nicholson and his compeers won their reputations and formed their characters. If we remember that the men who served in India during these years often felt that they were exterminating vermin, and that they were flung widely over newly conquered territory where their authority was almost entirely personal and their power enormous, the ruthlessness and spiritual arrogance with which our people confronted the Mutiny become explicable, and there is the less reason for the whitewashing of our text-books and their extraordinary moral judgments. The Panjab administration, before and after, as well as during, the Mutiny, was terribly stern. These years of suppression of inhumanities and of conquest and subjugation, after the explosion of 1857 threw a wild storm-light over all our thinking, produced the hard, unattractive English life in India which our novelists, consciously and unconsciously, have so successfully made us realize. That life was perhaps the most cynical (and yet confidently righteous) and least humorous phase in all our history as a people.

I am not justifying anything that happened; I am trying to explain; and I do not believe that to explain is to justify. Between 1830 and 1880 a beneficial ruthlessness was busy, and a self-satisfaction and an isolation from the people of India reigned. If I would see the writing of Indian history a franker, less cautious thing, and salted with a magnanimous and less narrowly political philosophy, it is because this would go far towards winning the interest of my people, who are weary both of the querulous plaints of Indians and of the angry pompousness of our own satraps and apologists. I believe, too, that another long step towards winning interest will be taken if we can arrest some of the excessive attention that has been given to the men prominent in 1857 and later years and turn it towards the able and generous men who worked in India in the period immediately before the great annexations and the great rebellion—towards Munro, Malcolm, Elphinstone, Tod.

### The Psychology of the "Satīs."

I had intended to try to examine this; but the truth is, it has ceased to seem a puzzle to me. Obviously the mental state of the women who were sacrificed varied infinitely, as that of martyrs for religion or patriotism. The Rajput lady who died when a foe girdled in her city and her whole sex was swept away, or who ascended the pyre with her lord newly slain in battle, was in a mood that had no contact or resemblance with the mood of the cowed and unwilling slave-girl. Yet even Rajput queens ultimately refused to go to the pyre.

Indians cherish with a rapture of exultation their many stories of *satīs* who died calmly or with lofty ecstasy. Those who saw Dip Kunwar, "the last distinguished *satī* in Bikanir," go to her death in 1825 spoke of her radiant heroism as long as they lived. Yet, after all, even such cases as this are only examples of what the history of every country has shown—that men and women, not only separately but in the mass, can be disciplined and trained to an extent to which no limit can be set. Soldiers, members of communities dedicated to destruction—as some warrior tribes and sects have been in times of national despair—slaves, the labouring classes during the long industrial depression now slowly lifting—all these have been trained to accept without question a fate that to sober thought is horrible. It is but a few years since men of almost every nation in Europe were disciplined to the point that they would accept a command to go to inevitable death with resignation or even joy. Women especially have shown a power of passive acceptance of a drab and colourless plane of existence in which their personality was crushed out of even a claim for recognition, that may be to their credit—I am by no means sure that it is—but is certainly not to that of man. That large sections of Indian society trained their women to look forward to the funeral pyre of their lord as the crown and glory of their lives is true. It is true also that to this day many Indian women cherish a sentimental worship of that mood, in which their menfolk encourage them, and that the writer who lays the facts in sunlight and thereby slays the ignoble and slavish folly that has given them so much satisfaction will receive only resentment. Nevertheless, the discipline that made suttee possible was a discipline of slaves; and the civilization that hounded widows, in the first moments of grief or surprise, into a declaration that they would die, and then forbade any withdrawal, was a barbarous one.

### Would Suttee revive if the British left India?

Not as an established custom—at any rate, not where the nationalist movement connected with the name of Mr. Gandhi has been strong. For that movement has been a cleansing one, since it has brought with it the deepest and most radical criticism to which Indians have ever submitted themselves; it has loosened a great many things, besides the British hold on India.

But there would undoubtedly be instances of suttee, especially where Brahman or Rajput influence is strong;

and in some districts the rite might become not uncommon. The disquieting thing is, suttee has troubled the Hindu conscience hardly at all. Even a saint such as Kabir mentions it with detachment, as an illustration of his theme, the extent to which love, whether of a husband or of God, can move those it possesses.

Yet, as European history has shown, it is not fair to expect even saints to be in all ethical questions in advance of their age. What we *are* entitled to consider strange is that, while some Indian writers whom the West has deeply influenced—for example, Romesh Dutt and Rajendralal Mitra—have condemned suttee uncompromisingly, it is common—indeed, usual—for Hindu writers to glorify it to-day, and there is a widespread belief that it proved the superior chastity of their women. Suttee and nationalism are the two subjects on which the irony-loving Bengali is nearly always heavily and solemnly serious. The courage of the *satīs* appeals to something in even the most "advanced" Hindu that is absent from the normal-thinking person in the West, and that courage is the only thing that Indians have fixed their eyes on. It is at last worth while trying to draw attention to other aspects of the rite. The last few years have brought to the younger generation of Indians, especially those studying in the West, such a feeling of weakness and humiliation that they are anxious to be *right* in their thinking, and are ceasing to be sensitive lest a confession that they were mistaken in some matter lower their dignity with foreigners. The free man can face the opinion of others, for their condemnation is nothing to him unless his own conscience go along with it.

Indians are with reason resentful of much that is said on missionary platforms in Europe and America and in missionary journals. Missionary apologetics have stressed the weak points in Hinduism, and have brought to the comparison only the strength of Christianity, ignoring such matters as its stormy and poetic but chaotic and mistaken eschatology. India has a right to point out to her critics the materialism of Western civilization and Europe's record of aggression outside herself. The weakest thing in Hinduism is its ethical record, which is a shocikng one. There is no single instance of a cruelty or an injustice which the religion or the people have shaken off from within. Reform has always come by forcible interposition from without, and without that forcible interposition would never have come. If the positive programme of Mr. Gandhi is followed, in such matters as the removal of untouchability, this record of Hinduism will be for the first time broken.

The refusal to glorify the past where it was vile is the only course consistent with self-respect. It is also the only way to win the respect of the world and, I believe, the help of English men and women in the struggle for Indian self-determination. For it is one thing to recognize the abstract justice of a cause, and quite another to move to its assistance. Greece and Italy have been trumpet-calls to civilized men everywhere; India is usually only a *Ducdame*, and will be until more sense is talked by us who love her. It is possible for a civilization to spoil its women by adulation and by attaching importance to their silliest and most trivial opinions. But Indian civilization has spoiled its men, a fact written large on Indian literature, making much of its finest poetry and fiction unreadable outside India without contempt mingling with admiration. I am sure that in India generally, and in certain parts especially, the men have for millenniums accepted and commanded from the women more than they could afford to take. As a result, the thinking and imagination of peoples second to none intellectually have been largely sterile.

I believe the time is come for a much more radical sifting of Hindu tradition by Indians themselves; and they will be wise if they adjust their attitude to the past by one consideration only—that of truth, and if while doing this they forget that they are a dependent people and exposed to a galling criticism from outside. The criticism that matters is their own; and on this question, of woman's position in society and her duties towards man, that criticism has not been searching or brave enough. I have tried to make it as impossible for an educated Indian to defend suttee as it is now impossible for an educated

Englishman to defend execution by torture; and when the defence is abandoned, the contempt that the defending inspires will pass away. What is more important, once the light of honest thinking is let in on this sacrifice of woman, other ideas that have sheltered behind this idol will be dragged out to question. The nonsense about the wonderful purity and spirituality of the Hindu marriage ideal cannot survive examination; still less can the sex-obsession of the civilization and the social system which, in making one sex the unpitied servant to the other, drains and destroys both. If the matter is brought to the political test, which—not unnaturally—is what appeals most to educated Indians to-day, then we may say this: they have friends who gladly acknowledge their right to complete self-determination, yet cannot see what *use* freedom can be to them until the whole of their sex-thinking has been ruthlessly overhauled and the plain conclusions of reason and justice put in practice. Suttee has gone, but its background remains. Children are married and ravished, their bodies maimed, their minds mutilated. If a generation could arise with the physical and mental vigour that in nearly every other land is a normal possession, much that is now thought admirable in Hindu literature and religion would be seen as a revolting nightmare. There are communities free from man-worship and sex-obsession, such as the Brahmo Samaj and kindred Churches; but even these are dishonoured, and their humiliating sense of impotence deepened, by the inability of the vast majority of their fellow-countrymen to see anything amiss in Hindu civilization or anything that needs to be done in India except political agitation. If there is any "gulf" between East and West, it is where sex and the family are in question, and woman's function and her relation to man. India cherishes some exquisite stories of wedded love. But if even the tales of Sita and Savitri and Damayanti, or—to bring the matter on to the plane of history—those of Dip Kunwar and the gallant ladies who burned for Prithviraj and Sardar Shan Singh, represent the whole or the best of what they can conceive of the comradeship of man and woman, then there is a gulf between East and West indeed.

# APPENDIX

## SOME ACCOUNTS OF SUTTEE

B.C. 317. "Finally, having taken leave of those of the household, she was set upon the pyre by her own brother, and was regarded with wonder by the crowd that had run together to the spectacle, and heroically ended her life, the whole force with their arms thrice marching round the pyre before it was kindled. But she, laying herself beside her husband, and even at the violence of the flame giving utterance to no unbecoming cry, stirred pity indeed in others of the spectators, and in some excess of eulogy; not but what there were some of the Greeks present who reprobated such rites as barbarous and cruel."[1] (In the Panjab.)

*Circa* A.D. 1520. "They hold that the wife who weeps beyond measure has no desire to go in search of her husband; and the mourning finished, their relations speak to them, advising them to burn themselves and not to dishonour their generation. After that, it is said, they place the dead man on a bed with a canopy of branches and covered with flowers, and they put the woman on the back of a worthless horse, and she goes after them with many jewels on her and covered with roses; she carries a mirror in her hand and in the other a branch of flowers, and (she goes accompanied by) many kinds of music, and his relations (go with her) with much pleasure. A man goes also playing on a small drum, and he sings songs to her telling her that she is going to join her husband, and she answers also in singing that so she will do. As soon as she arrives at the place where they

[1] Diodorus Siculus, *Biblioth.*, xix. 33–4. Quoted in *Hobson-Jobson*, article "Suttee."

are always burned, she waits with the musicians till her husband is burned." [1] (In the Vijayanagar Empire.)

"About the year 1796 the following most shocking and atrocious murder, under the name of *suhu-murunu*, was perpetrated at Mujil-poori, about a day's journey south from Calcutta. Bancharamu, a bramhun of the above place, dying, his wife went to be burnt with the body. All the previous ceremonies were performed; she was fastened on the pile, and the fire was kindled; but the night was dark and rainy. When the fire began to scorch this poor woman, she contrived to disentangle herself from the dead body and, creeping from under the pile, hid herself among some brush-wood. In a little time it was discovered that there was only one body on the pile. The relations immediately took the alarm and searched for the poor wretch; the son soon dragged her forth, and insisted that she should throw herself on the pile again, or drown or hang herself. She pleaded for her life at the hands of her own son, and declared that she could not embrace so horrid a death—but she pleaded in vain. The son urged that he should lose his caste, and therefore he would die, or she should. Unable to persuade her to hang or drown herself, the son and the others present then tied her hands and feet and threw her on the funeral pile, where she quickly perished." [2]

1813. "The following circumstance took place at Gondul-para, about twenty miles north of Calcutta, on the 18th of March, 1813, and was communicated to the author by Captain Kemp, an eye-witness. The description is nearly in his own words: 'On Thursday last, at nine in the morning, Vishwunat'hu, one of our best workmen, who had been sick but a short time, was brought down to the river-side to expire. He was placed, as is customary, on the bank, and a consultation held respecting the time he would die; the

[1] *Chronicle of Ferñao Nuniz*, published in Sewell's *Forgotten Empire*. As Longhurst remarks (*Hampi Ruins*, 41), Nuniz's extraordinarily vivid account, of which part has been quoted earlier, must be based on personal experience.

[2] William Ward, *A View of the History, Literature and Mythology of the Hindoos* (1822), iii. 316–17.

astrologer predicted that his dissolution was near at hand. The sick man was then immersed up to the middle in the river, and there kept for some time; but death not being so near as was predicted, he was again placed on the beach, extended at full length, and exposed to a hot sun, where he continued the whole of the day, excepting at those intervals when it was supposed he was dying, when he was again immersed in the sacred stream. I visited him in the evening; he was sensible, but had not the power of utterance. He, however, was able to make signs with his hand that he did not wish to drink the river water, which they kept almost continually pouring into his mouth by means of a small shell. He remained in this situation during the night. In the morning the immersions commenced, and were continued at intervals till about five in the evening, when he expired, or was literally murdered. His wife, a young woman about sixteen years of age, hearing of his death, came to the desperate resolution of being buried alive with the corpse. She was accompanied by her friends down to the beach where the body lay, where a small branch of the mango tree was presented to her, which (as I understood) was a setting a seal to her determination, from which, after having accepted the branch, she could not retreat. I went to her, and questioned her with respect to the horrid act she was about to perform, whether it was voluntary or from persuasion. Nothing of the latter appeared; it was entirely her own desire. . . . The mother declared that it was her daughter's choice, who added that she was determined to "go the road her husband had gone." There was not the least appearance of regret observable in the mother's countenance or conduct. . . . At 8 p.m. the corpse, accompanied by this self-devoted victim, was conveyed to a place a little below our grounds, where I repaired, to behold the perpetration of a crime which I could scarcely believe possible to be committed by any human being. The corpse was laid on the earth by the river till a circular grave of about fifteen feet in circumference and five or six feet deep was prepared, and was then (after some formulas had been read) placed at the bottom of the grave in a sitting posture, with the face to the north, the nearest relation applying a lighted wisp of straw to the top of the head. The young widow now came forward, and having circumambulated the grave seven times, calling out "Huree Bul! Huree Bul!" in which she was joined by the surrounding crowd, descended into it. I then approached within a foot of the grave, to observe if any reluctance appeared in her countenance or sorrow in that of her relations. In hers no alteration was perceptible; in theirs was the appearance of exultation. She placed herself in a sitting posture, with her face to the back of her husband, embracing the corpse with her left arm and reclining her head on his shoulders; the other hand she placed over her own head, with her forefinger erect, which she moved in a circular direction. The earth was then deliberately put round them, two men being in the grave for the purpose of stamping it round the living and the dead, which they did as a gardener does around a plant newly transplanted, till the earth rose to a level with the surface, or two or three feet above the heads of the entombed. As her head was covered some time before the finger of the right hand, I had an opportunity of observing whether any regret was manifested; but the finger moved round in the same manner as at first, till the earth closed the scene. Not a parting tear was observed to be shed by any of her relations till the crowd began to disperse, when the usual lamentations and howling commenced, without sorrow.'"[1]

*June* 9, 1826. "About five o'clock in the evening of the 9th instant I received a note from a gentleman that a suttee was about to take place near his house. On hastening to the spot, I found the preparations considerably advanced, and a large concourse of spectators assembled, and continually increasing, till they amounted to six or eight thousand. On my left stood a horrid pile. It was an oblong bed of dry cow-dung cakes about ten feet long and seven wide and three high. At each end of it a rough stake about eight feet in length was driven into the ground, and at about a foot from the top of these supporters was fastened, by cords, a frame of the same dimensions as the bed below, and forming a flat canopy to the couch of death. This frame must have been of considerable weight, as it was covered

[1] Ward, iii, 324–26.

with very dry small faggots, which the officiating Brahmuns continued to throw upon it till they rose two feet above the framework. On the right sat the poor deluded widow, who was to be the victim of this heart-rending display of Hindoo purity and gentleness. She was attended by a dozen or more Brahmuns; her mother, sister, and son, an interesting boy about three years of age, and other relatives were also with her. Her own infant, not twelve months old, was craftily kept from her by the Brahmuns. She had already performed a number of preparatory ceremonies, one of which was washing herself in a strong decoction of saffron, which is supposed to have a purifying effect. One effect it certainly produced: it imparted to her a horrid ghastliness; her eyes indicated a degree of melancholy wildness; a forced and unnatural smile now and then played on her countenance; and, indeed, everything about her person and her conduct indicated that narcotics had been administered in no small quantities. She was clad in her best apparel, which had been tinted by the same decoction with which her body—alas! so soon to be fuel for the flames—had been washed. Her jewels for the last time were employed to ornament her person; in her fine long black hair at the back of her head, as in a bag of network, were enclosed so large a quantity of small white odoriferous flowers as almost to prevent her head from being turned; and about two yards from where the unfortunate woman sat, immediately in her view, was the corpse of her husband, tied by a cord to a kind of hurdle made of bamboos. Her attention, however, so far as I could observe, was never, even for a moment, directed towards it. To divert her thoughts from dwelling on the scene around her, and in which she was shortly to become so conspicuous an object, and doubtless to prevent her resolution from failing her at the approaching crisis, the Brahmuns continued plying her with betel-leaf, plantains, cocoa-nuts, etc., etc., to distribute among her friends as presents; and the manner in which these presents were received sufficiently evinced the almost divine regard with which the giver was contemplated. Besides these different kinds of fruits, several small brass pans filled with parched rice, sandal-wood powder, etc., were before her. From these she occasionally distributed to the Brahmuns or distinguished individuals by pinches of their contents; and the receivers of these presents appeared to consider them as peculiarly precious. When, however, an interval, though but momentary, occurred amidst these employments, her countenance assumed an expression that indicated indescribable apprehension and horror.

"Close by me stood the Fouzdar, a native officer, who, besides regulating the police, is the chief military officer at the station. Under his authority and personal superintendence this inhuman business was carrying on. So heartily did he engage in the murderous work that he gave the poor widow twenty pagodas—between six and seven pounds sterling—to confirm her resolution to be burned!

"All my hopes of prevailing on the widow to retract her rash vow and openly to declare her determination not to burn were precluded, as she was a Gentoo woman, of whose language I had no knowledge. Happily, however, Mr. Campbell, of the London Missionary Society, was present, and with the hope that she would understand him he advanced to address her in the Carnatica language. His attempt in this respect was successful, for, notwithstanding the prohibition of the Fouzdar, he succeeded in getting near enough to her for her to hear his address; and from the attention she paid to what he said and the fact of her answering it was evident that she understood him. The effect of Mr. Campbell's solemn and feeling address was counteracted by the influence and exhortations of the Brahmuns, who surrounded their victim like so many beasts of prey, fearful of its escaping their grasp; and he was obliged to retire, without having effected anything more than to exhibit the striking contrast which exists between the spirit of the Gospel of Our Blessed Lord and that of what has often been termed 'mild and amicable' Hindooism.

"By this time the pile was completed, and a quantity of straw was now spread on the top of the bed of cow-dung cakes. An increase of activity was soon visible among the men whose 'feet are so swift to shed blood.' Muntrams (prayers or incantations) having been repeated over the pile and the woman, and everything being in readiness, the hurdle to which the corpse of the husband had been fastened was now raised by six of the officiating Brahmuns; the end of a cord about two yards long, attached at the other end to the head of the bier, was taken by the widow, and the whole moved slowly towards the pile. The corpse was then laid on the right side upon the straw, with which it was covered, and four men furnished with sharp swords, one stationed at each corner, now drew them from their scabbards. The trembling, ghastly offering to the Moloch of Hindooism then began her seven circuits round the fatal pile, and finally halted opposite to her husband's corpse, at the left side of it, where she was evidently greatly agitated. Here five or six Brahmuns began to talk to her with much vehemence, till, in a paroxysm of desperation, assisted by the Brahmuns, the hopeless widow ascended the bed of destruction. Her mother and her sister, unable any longer to sustain the extremity of their anguish, went up to the side of the pile and entreated that the horrid purpose might be abandoned; but the woman, fearing the encounter and the strength of her resolution, without uttering a word or even casting a parting glance at her supplicating parent and sister, threw herself down on the pile and clasped the half-putrid corpse in her arms. Straw in abundance was then heaped on the dead and the living; gums, resins and other inflammable materials were thrown upon the straw which covered the bodies by one party of the Brahmuns, while muntrams were repeated at their heads by the other. Six or eight pieces of kindled cow-dung cakes were introduced among the straw at different parts of the pile, ghee and inflammable materials were applied, and the whole blazed in as many places. The men with swords at each corner then hacked the cords which supported the flat canopy of faggots—it fell and covered the lifeless corpse and the living woman!!!

"The flames now began to ascend, and comparative silence was restored. The active agents in this work of destruction were fearlessly and explicitly charged with murder and warned of the future awful account which they would have to render. The Fouzdar, in a haughty, irritated tone of voice, inquired, 'To whom shall I have to give an account?' He was informed, 'To Jehovah, the true and living God.' To the charge of murdering the widow and hurrying her soul to perdition, the chief Brahmun, in a frenzy of enthusiastic triumph, exclaimed, accompanying what he said with the most extravagant gesticulations: 'She is now in heaven —she is already in glory!' At this moment a piercing sound caught my ear; I listened a few seconds, and, notwithstanding the noise of the multitude, heard the shrieks of misery which issued from the burning pile!! In an agony of feeling we directed the attention of the Brahmuns to this, and while doing so, again, still louder and more piercing than before, the burning woman rent the air with her shrieks!! Several of the Brahmuns called out to the half-consumed, still conscious and imploring widow to comfort her. What the real effect on the mind of this wretched victim to Hindoo infatuation would be is easily conceived. They then sang in chorus a Sanscrita hymn declaring that her soul would be wafted to heaven on the zephyrs of their holy praise. The pile was now enveloped in flames, and so intense was the heat that, as by one consent, the Brahmuns and the spectators retreated several paces; and the hymn ended, but not the shrieks and groans of the agonized sufferer: they still pierced our ears and almost rent our hearts! Effectually to overpower them, the Brahmuns in a body began calling aloud, 'Rayana![1] Rayana! Rayana!' (one of the thousand names of Vishnu). Scarcely conscious of what I did, in the midst of these vain repetitions I left this scene of fiendish barbarity."[2] (At Bangalore, Mysore.)

"On Tuesday, November 24, 1829, I had an application from the heads of the most respectable and most extensive family of Brahmans in this district to suffer this old woman to burn herself with the remains of her husband, Ummed Singh Upadhya, who had that morning died upon the banks of the Nerbudda. I threatened to enforce my order and punish severely any man who assisted, and placed a police guard for the purpose of seeing that no one did so. She remained sitting by the edge of the water without eating or drinking. The next day the body of her husband was burned to ashes in a small pit of about eight feet square

[1] *Nārāyana.*

[2] *Missionary Notices*, No. xxviii, June 1827. The letter is prefaced, "Mr. England dates his letter June 12, 1826."

and three or four feet deep, before several thousand spectators who had assembled to see the suttee. All strangers dispersed before evening, as there seemed to be no prospect of my yielding to the urgent solicitations of her family. . . . She remained sitting on a bare rock in the bed of the Nerbudda, refusing every kind of sustenance and exposed to the intense heat of the sun by day and the severe cold of the night, with only a thin sheet thrown over her shoulders. On Thursday, to cut off all hope of her being moved from her purpose, she put on the *dhajā*, or coarse red turban, and broke her bracelets in pieces, by which she became dead in law and for ever excluded from caste. Should she choose to live after this, she could never return to her family. . . . I became satisfied that she would starve herself to death if not allowed to burn, by which the family would be disgraced, her miseries prolonged, and I myself rendered liable to be charged with a wanton abuse of authority, for no prohibition of the kind I had issued has as yet received the formal sanction of the Government.[1]

"On Saturday, the 28th, in the morning, I rode out ten miles to the spot, and found the poor old widow sitting with the *dhajā* round her head, a brass plate before her with undressed rice and flowers, and a cocoa-nut in each hand. She talked very collectedly, telling me that 'she had determined to mix her ashes with those of her departed husband, and should patiently wait my permission to do so, assured that God would enable her to sustain life till that was given, though she dared not eat or drink.' Looking at the sun, then rising before her over a long and beautiful reach of the Nerbudda river, she said calmly: 'My soul has been for five days with my husband's near that sun; nothing but my earthly frame is left; and this I know you will in time suffer to be mixed with the ashes of his in yonder pit, because it is not in your nature or usage wantonly to prolong the miseries of a poor old woman.'

[1] Sleeman, on taking civil charge of the Jabalpur district, in March 1828, issued a proclamation forbidding anyone from aiding or assisting in suttee, saying that if a woman burned with her husband anyone who provided wood for his pyre would be liable to punishment.

"'Indeed, it is not. My object and duty is to save and preserve them; and I am come to dissuade you from this idle purpose, to urge you to live, and to keep your family from the disgrace of being thought your murderers.'

"'I am not afraid of their ever being so thought; they have all, like good children, done everything in their power to induce me to live among them, and, if I had done so, I know they would have loved and honoured me. But my duties to them have now ended. I commit them all to your care, and I go to attend my husband, *Ummed Singh Upadhya*, with whose ashes on the funeral pile mine have been already three times mixed.'[1]

"This was the first time in her long life that she had ever pronounced the name of her husband, for in India no woman, high or low, ever pronounces the name of her husband—she would consider it disrespectful towards him to do so. . . . When the old lady named her husband, as she did with strong emphasis and in a very deliberate manner, everyone present was satisfied that she had resolved to die. 'I have,' she continued, 'tasted largely of the bounty of Government, having been maintained by it with all my large family in ease and comfort upon our rent-free lands, and I feel assured that my children will not be suffered to want; but with them I have nothing more to do, our intercourse and communion here end. My soul (*prān*) is with *Ummed Singh Upadhya*, and my ashes must here mix with his.'

"Again looking to the sun: 'I see them together,' said she, with a tone and countenance that affected me a good deal, 'under the bridal canopy!'—alluding to the ceremonies of marriage; and I am satisfied that she at that moment really believed that she saw her own spirit and that of her husband under the bridal canopy in paradise.

"I tried to work upon her pride and her fears. I told her that it was probable that the rent-free lands by which her family had been so long supported might be resumed by the Government, as a mark of its displeasure against the children for not dissuading her from the sacrifice; that the temples over her ancestors upon the bank might be levelled

[1] It was a common belief of a widow that she had died as a *satī* previously with her husband.

with the ground, in order to prevent their operating to induce others to make similar sacrifices; and lastly, that not one single brick or stone should ever mark the place where she died if she persisted in her resolution. But, if she consented to live, a splendid habitation should be built for her among these temples, a handsome provision assigned for her support out of these rent-free lands, her children should come daily to visit her, and I should frequently do the same. She smiled, but held out her arm and said: 'My pulse has long ceased to beat, my spirit has departed, and I have nothing left but a little *earth* that I wish to mix with the ashes of my husband. I shall suffer nothing in burning, and, if you wish proof, order some fire, and you shall see this arm consumed without giving me any pain.' I did not attempt to feel her pulse, but some of my people did, and declared that it had ceased to be perceptible. At this time every native present believed that she was incapable of suffering pain, and her end confirmed them in their opinion.

"Satisfied myself that it would be unavailing to attempt to save her life, I sent for all the principal members of the family, and consented that she should be suffered to burn herself if they would enter into engagements that no other member of their family should ever do the same. This they all agreed to, and the papers having been drawn out in due form about midday, I sent down notice to the old lady, who seemed extremely pleased and thankful. The ceremonies of bathing were gone through before three, while the wood and other combustible materials for a strong fire were collected and put into the pit. After bathing, she called for a *pān* (betel leaf) and ate it; then rose up and, with one arm on the shoulder of her eldest son and the other on that of her nephew, approached the fire. I had sentries placed all round, and no other person was allowed to approach within five paces. As she rose up fire was set to the pile, and it was instantly in a blaze. The distance was about one hundred and fifty yards. She came on with a calm and cheerful countenance, stopped once, and, casting her eyes upward, said: 'Why have they kept me five days from thee, my husband?' On coming to the sentries her supporters stopped; she walked once round the pit, paused a moment, and, while muttering a prayer, threw some flowers into the fire. She then walked up deliberately and steadily to the brink, stepped into the centre of the flame, sat down, and, leaning back in the midst as if reposing upon a couch, was consumed without uttering a shriek or betraying one sign of agony.

"A few instruments of music had been provided, and they played as usual as she approached the fire, not, as is commonly supposed, in order to drown screams, but to prevent the last words of the victim from being heard, as these are supposed to be prophetic and might become sources of pain or strife to the living. It was not expected that I should yield, and but few people had assembled to witness the sacrifice, so that there was little or nothing in the circumstances immediately around to stimulate her to any extraordinary exertions; and I am persuaded that it was the desire of again being united to her husband in the next world and the entire confidence that she would be so if she now burned herself that alone sustained her. From the morning he died (Tuesday) till Wednesday evening she ate *pāns*, or betel leaves, but nothing else; and from Wednesday evening she ceased eating them. She drank no water from Tuesday. She went into the fire with the same cloth about her that she had worn in the bed of the river; but it was made wet from a persuasion that even the shadow of any impure thing falling upon her from going to the pile contaminates the woman unless counteracted by the sheet moistened in the holy stream.

"I must do the family the justice to say that they all exerted themselves to dissuade the widow from her purpose. . . ."[1]

1839. "Her countenance had assumed a sickly and ghastly appearance, which was partly owing to internal agitation and partly, so I was informed, to the effects of opium and bhang and other narcotics, with which she had been previously drugged in order to render her less awake

[1] Major-General Sir W. H. Sleeman, *Rambles and Recollections of an Indian Official* (1893 edition, Constable), i. 23–28.

to the misery of her situation. She was not, however, so insensible to what was passing as to be inattentive to two persons in particular amongst several others who were stooping before her and were evidently imploring her blessing. . . .

"In about half an hour the preparations were completed. She was regularly thatched in upon the top of the pile, whilst her husband's body yet lay outside. It was finally lifted up to her; the head as usual, and which is the most interesting part of the ceremony, was received upon her lap. . . .

"The woman became a *satī* when she crossed the threshold of her door, and would most probably (so I was told) have been put to death by her relations had she afterwards retreated. So long as she remained in the house she had the power of refusal." [1] (In Mandi.)

*November* 5, 1845. "I have just returned from a suttee; after twenty years' residence in India this is the first I have seen. A terrible sight, but less so than I expected. The woman was cool and collected, and evidently under no sort of coercion. The corpse was that of a Goorkha commandant; it was laid on a small platform, raised on six or eight stakes driven into an island, eight or nine feet square, in the bed of the Bagmutty. The platform had a double bottom; between the two was laid wood, resin, and ghee; the corner stakes met above, forming a rude canopy. About a hundred spectators, chiefly beggars and old women, were collected to view the spectacle. Ten or twelve Sepoys and as many Brahmins were assisting around the pile. When Dr. Christie and I arrived the woman was inside a small (open) rattee close to the river, apparently dressing; we could just see her tinsel head-dress. In about five minutes she came out mounted on the back of a man. At the edge of the rattee her carrier stopped, and she, dipping her finger in a platter, took red dye stuff and made *teekas* on the foreheads of some of the assistants. He then carried her to the pile, and round it four or five times, during which time she took rice and spices from a platter and threw it to the people around, who held out their hands, and many their sheets, to catch

[1] G. T. Vigne, *Travels in Kashmir, Ladak, Iskardo*, 82–3.

it; others begged for alms and her ornaments. Two or three tomtoms were all the time being beat. After finishing the circuits, she dismounted, stooped, and washed her hands in the river, and then uncovered her husband's feet, placed her head to them, and kissed them. She then ascended the pile, made more distributions of rice, etc., and some pice, and commenced disrobing herself, taking off her tiara and upper coloured silks, and gave them to persons around. She then sat down and took off her armlets and bracelets and gave them. All this took at least a quarter of an hour, during which time she was as composed as at a festival. She then lay down close behind the corpse, her head close to her husband's. The platform was so narrow that she had to be squeezed between the corpse and the stakes on her side. Her hair throughout was loose, hanging over her shoulder. She was a Goorkha, about thirty-five or forty years old. When laid down, the coloured sheet over her husband was drawn so as to cover her too, and then three strong bamboos were placed across the pair, and each held at either end by a man so as to prevent her rising. They did not press on her, but would have effectually kept her down had she struggled. Over these bamboos some loose faggots were thrown, and then two lighted lamp-wicks were placed on the head of the corpse; and a minute after a torch was applied under the platform close to the heads, when a strong flame broke out. The crowd shouted and the tomtoms beat more loudly so as to have drowned any cry that may have been uttered by the victim; but whatever were her pains, they could not have lasted a minute. The fire was fed with ghee and sulphur, and a strong flame kept up so as in five minutes to have quite consumed all the head of the platform. I have seen the sad spectacle, and shall not willingly witness another. The old hags around me grinned with delight; ours were the only sad countenances. I saw two or three women near the victim who were probably relations, but such could not be known from their actions; all was utter unconcern." (In Nepal. Sir Henry Lawrence's *Diary*.)[1]

[1] Sir Herbert Benjamin Edwardes and Herman Merivale, *Life of Sir Henry Lawrence* (1872), ii. 36–7.

# INDEX